# Making Rural Buildings
# FOR MODEL RAILWAYS

D1194665

# Making Rural Buildings
# FOR MODEL RAILWAYS

David Wright

THE CROWOOD PRESS

First published in 2013 by
The Crowood Press Ltd
Ramsbury, Marlborough
Wiltshire SN8 2HR

**www.crowood.com**

**British Library Cataloguing-in-Publication Data**
A catalogue record for this book is available from the British Library.

ISBN 978 1 84797 460 0

**Dedication**
I would like to dedicate this book to my good friend Dave Richards.
Dave has always supported me, giving me encouragement with my
model making. He is also credited with originating a good number of the
photographic images in this book, for which I am very grateful.

Front cover image: A scene from the mill on the author's layout
Tawcombe. Photo: Steve Flint, courtesy of *Railway Modeller* magazine.

Back cover centre image: A Great Western Star class is seen passing
Pendon Parva signal box, on Pendon Museum's Vale of White Horse model.
The buildings and scenics are modelled to perfection on what must surely
be the finest model railway around today! Photograph from the Pendon
Collection, reproduced here by the kind permission of Pendon Museum.

Frontispiece image by Dave Richards.

Typeset by Servis Filmsetting Ltd., Stockport, Cheshire
Printed and bound in India by Replika Press Ltd

# CONTENTS

# PREFACE

From as long as I can remember, I have had an interest in making things. This interest has combined with an ability to observe things around me. From a very early age I would find myself recording what I saw, by making rough sketches. My father always encouraged me and indeed I must have inherited some of his artistic skills, as he was a talented artist himself. He also had a talent to design and make useful items for the home, which again must have rubbed off on my young mind. Like most young boys growing up in the fifties and sixties, I was bought a train set for a Christmas present. The first was a Hornby clockwork, set up on the living room floor. Then a few years later I was given a Tri-ang TT train set. This time my father and elder brother had fixed the layout down to a large baseboard with scenery. I remember it vividly as it gave me many hours of pleasure.

It was not long before I found myself wanting to add more buildings to the layout. My father saw my interest and bought me a card cottage kit. With his help, I made my first model building, thus setting the seeds of my future interest. From this beginning, many more buildings were to be constructed from the card Bilt-Ezee range. I remember making regular visits to the local model shop in Derby to select the next one to build. However, it would not be long before I started to design my own buildings using the card fold-up technique. My mother would save any cereal packaging for me to draw out and construct my first scratch-built efforts. At the same time as the visits to the model shop, my father would take me to see the wonderful O gauge 'Kirtley' Midland model railway exhibit, then housed in the Derby Museum. This model made a lasting impression on my young

*Aged six with my father at the 1962 Derby Locomotive Works Open Day. Railways, both full size and in miniature, were always a part of this young boy's life.* Photo: Colin Wright

*'Washgate Barn' was the first commissioned model building that I constructed for the Midland Railway exhibit housed in the Silk Mill, Derby. This layout is a rebuild of the original model of 'Kirtley', which had proved such an inspiration for me as a boy.* Photo: Jeff Mander

mind, always being impressed with the quality of the buildings and scenery this layout displayed. Little did I know then that forty years on, I would be constructing the buildings for the rebuilt version of 'Kirtley', now housed in the Silk Mill, Derby's former Museum of Industry. Through my teenage years other interests were soon to take over, like girls, pop music, football and so on.

My artistic ability was to give me a career as a graphic designer and illustrator. From time to time the job would involve model making, such as creating models of exhibition stands for companies exhibiting their products and services at the National Exhibition Centre. My interest in model railways was rekindled after I was invited along by a work colleague to the local Model Railway Club. The interest from those early years was soon revived with the desire to create a layout and replicate the buildings of the selected area on which I based my model railway. My interest was extended with a visit to Pendon Museum in Oxfordshire. The quality of the model buildings and scenery, representing rural Britain in the 1920s and 1930s, is exceptional and I would strongly recommend a visit. The buildings on display certainly gave me the inspiration to

improve my scratch buildings and it became my benchmark to achieve something like the standards seen at Pendon. I hope by reading this book, you too will be inspired to have a go at creating some of our rural buildings for your model railway and have the satisfaction of building something you can be proud of.

The hobby of model railways is probably stronger now than it has ever been. This is evident from the amount of exhibitions around the country and the thousands of people visiting them. It is also true that most of us strive to achieve higher standards in our models. The market has never been better, especially for off-the-shelf examples. The amount of detail that can now be reproduced on an out-of-the-box model is truly amazing. Anybody just starting out, or getting back into the hobby, will be spoilt for choice with all the locomotives, rolling stock and, of course, the buildings that are now available. The scratch-builder, however, has not been left out completely. There is also an increasing range of materials and accessories available to help give you plenty of scope to build a good model.

Model railways have always been a good platform for learning and trying out new skills. Indeed, the

*The 7mm Midland Railway exhibit, housed in the Silk Mill, Derby's Museum of Industry. The water tower and the nearest station buildings were all built by the author as commissions.* Photo: Jeff Mander

hobby includes carpentry for baseboard construction, electronics for wiring, engineering for locomotive building – the list goes on. For me, though, the most enjoyable part of the hobby is the artistic element, whereby perhaps we can allow ourselves to be a little more imaginative and not be too concerned about the constraints that other areas of the hobby might demand. The skills required to achieve a reasonable standard when creating a building are achievable for the beginner, so long as you are prepared to take your time and always observe the world around you.

There is no reason at all why you should not be rewarded with convincing results.

Reading this book, and following the techniques and suggestions I have given, you should achieve something towards that goal. Remember that the main object of any hobby is to learn new things and, most importantly, to have fun doing it. The aim of this book is to provide you with the information, ideas and inspiration to be more creative when modelling rural buildings and to achieve a final result you can be justly proud of.

*The small Prairie Tank 4550 pulls away from Tawcombe Station, past the allotments. This is the author's own 4mm layout depiction of the rural Devonshire landscape in the 1930s.* Photo: Steve Flint, courtesy of Railway Modeller *magazine*

# CHAPTER ONE

# THE HISTORY OF RURAL BUILDINGS IN BRITAIN

Before we start to look at how we are going to construct models of our rural buildings, we need first to consider the history behind them. It is important to have some knowledge of how buildings have developed over the years and how different materials have been used to construct them. This will prove to be a valuable benefit when you come to build miniature versions for your model railway.

## THE RURAL SETTING

In this country we are blessed to have such a diverse range of rural buildings. The reason for this is down to geography and the geology of the land. Most of our rural buildings will have been constructed from the local materials, giving them the distinct style and character of that particular region. We can identify what part of the UK we are in just by looking at the buildings found there; for instance, if we see cottages constructed of a golden ochre limestone we know that we are in the Cotswolds.

If we go back in history we will find that the population of Britain depended on the countryside for its existence. Small settlements started to grow up around areas of forest that had been cleared to work the land. These early farmers built themselves primitive shelters, which they shared with their livestock. In some cases, these settlements would grow to form small hamlets that would become the basis for our rural villages.

Up until the seventeenth and eighteenth centuries, the majority of people lived and worked in the countryside, where the villages developed into open and closed examples. Open settlements grew either around industrial workings, or on common land. The closed settlements were under the tighter control of the Lord of the Manor and the haphazard building of homes was restricted to a more uniformed architectural style and layout. More substantial materials and building techniques started to be used. These dramatic changes came about with the introduction of the Enclosures Acts, the majority of which

*Our Iron Age ancestors worked the land and reared livestock. They built circular houses, seen here in a recreation of a Celtic Village at St Fagans National History Museum in Wales.*

were passed between 1750 and 1860 and gradually eroded the rights of local people to cultivate or graze animals on what had been common land. The Lord of the Manor would have a large country house built, serving as a status symbol of his wealth and importance. The house would be built a fair distance away from the villages and would be surrounded by parkland. The farmhouse also started to make its appearance into the British landscape.

More changes took place with the introduction of transportation and the formation of the Turnpike Trusts between the seventeenth and nineteenth centuries, which saw tolls collected for maintenance of roads. These roads would start to criss-cross the countryside, linking villages together. Before this, the only connections were rough drovers' tracks, used by farmers to move livestock to and from market.

In the second half of the eighteenth century, canals started to appear, linking towns with the countryside. Canals then gave way to the railways, which made the biggest impression. Now materials could be transported quickly around the country and new materials could be used to build or make improvements to rural buildings.

# BUILDING MATERIALS: WALLS

We can now look at the materials used to construct rural buildings, starting with the walls.

## TIMBER

The dwellings of the early settlements used wood for a basic framework. Thin strips of wood from hazel or willow, known as wattle, were then added, which would then be plastered in a clay mix known as daub. Later, more substantial frames started to be used. Two naturally curved branches would be selected from an oak tree and cut. These would be positioned to curve up to meet each other. This became a standard technique known as a 'cruck frame'. Examples of this type of frame can still be seen today.

Oak framing continued to be used, although the box frame method came to be preferred. The black and white half-timbered buildings we all love today were built in this way. This method of timbering has been revived over the last couple of centuries, although mainly for decoration rather than forming any structural importance.

The infill material used for the early timber-framed buildings was wattle and daub. This was a mixture of mud and clay bonded together with straw and

*This cottage, now rebuilt at St Fagans, has walls made from clay known locally as clom. The clay is mixed with straw and small stones, then laid in layers. A cruck frame supports the roof. The roof has a sub-base of wattle and gorse, which is then topped with straw thatch.*

A single-storey 'long house' built around 1508. This type of once-common farmhouse was created using a timber frame. The walls were covered in wattle and daub and finished with a lime wash. The roof is supported by a series of oak cruck 'A' frames. The long house is divided with accommodation for animals at one end. This rebuilt sample can be found at St Fagans National History Museum.

This photograph shows the construction of a cruck frame, discovered after demolition. It now is a feature in a wall located on St Mary's Gate, Wirksworth, Derbyshire.

The illustration (A) shows the construction of a cruck frame. The two curved oak frames are brought together at the apex. A cross beam of oak forms a letter 'A', giving the frame lateral strength. Illustration (B) shows the cruck frame exposed on the end of a cottage in Lacock, Wiltshire.

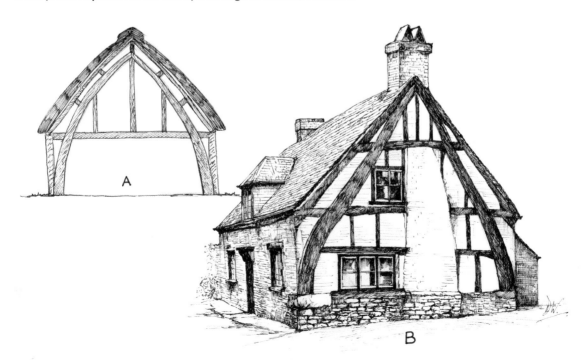

ABOVE: *An early timber-framed farmhouse of 1678, with a hipped roof of thatch. This rebuilt sample is at St Fagans National History Museum.*

BELOW: *This example of a grand half-timbered manor house is located at Somersal Herbert, near Ashbourne, south Derbyshire. It was built by John Fitzherbert in 1564.*

ABOVE: *Wakelyn Hall is an impressive manor house in Hilton, south Derbyshire. This half-timbered building has two wings using an 'H' footprint, which became a popular style for country houses in the early seventeenth century.*

BELOW: *A farmhouse constructed using a box timber frame with lath and plaster panels. This building still retains much of its original features at Doveridge, south Derbyshire.*

*The end elevation of the 1480s Grammar School in Ledbury, Herefordshire. This is a good example of a timber box frame with wooden mullion window frames.*

animal hair. Examples using this main building material can be seen in Devon, Somerset and Dorset, and is locally known as cob.

When brick became more popular, the daub infill for timber frames was replaced with this, although timber could also be used to clad frames. Shiplap weather boarding became a feature of buildings in the south-eastern counties of England, especially Suffolk, Essex, Sussex and Kent.

## STONE

Stone was used as a building material from early in history, although not originally for the humble dwelling. Stone would be used for its strength and for defence. From Roman times, stone masonry was used to construct defensive walls, forts and villas. The Romans brought amazing building skills to this country and we can still marvel at them today. Centuries of conflict and invasion led to the building of our castles and fortified manor houses. Stokesay

*The ruin of Throwley Old Hall stands overlooking the Manifold Valley in north Staffordshire. This Tudor manor house was built in 1503 using local limestone and non-local sandstone. The structure was built with defensive features to the walls.*

ABOVE: *This illustration of Fenny Bentley Hall in Derbyshire shows the defensive tower of the original hall, with the Tudor gables added at a later date.*

BELOW: *Built from local slate from North Wales, this was the home of a wealthy farmer. The building features unglazed timber mullion windows and two substantial chimneys. The farmhouse has been rebuilt at St Fagans National History Museum.*

*The ruin of the original gatehouse to Mackworth Castle in Derbyshire dates from 1500. Attached are later estate workers' cottages. This makes for an interesting combination of styles.*

in Shropshire is probably the best example of a fortified manor house. It also features a combination of the half-timbered box frame supported on a base of reinforced stone. Another feature was the tall square stone structure known as a pele tower. These were common in Wales and Northumbria and along the Scottish borders, where attack from 'reivers', savage border raiders, was still a threat.

Religious buildings started to appear, with stone being the preferred material. Churches, monasteries and abbeys graced our land. Gradually stone started to replace earlier materials for housing, farm buildings and country houses. Some of the stone would be recycled both from defensive structures and the monasteries after their dissolution from 1536 to 1541.

Local stone was quarried for most of our rural buildings; this was lightly dressed for parts of the building where strength mattered, like the corner quoins, lintels and sills. The rest was constructed using rubble as an infill and would be joined together

*Cilewent Farmhouse was originally built in 1470. This is the 1734 rebuild in the form of a long house. The local stone structure boasted a cow house with room for twelve cattle, a substantial hay loft, stables and a dairy all contained under the long slate-covered roof. It has been rebuilt at St Fagans National History Museum.*

*An unusual tall limestone-built outhouse in Wirksworth, Derbyshire. Its original use is not known, although it was probably used to store grain.*

with a lime mortar. In some cases, mortar would not be used at all, just being dry-stone built. The local stone used would give the distinct character to the buildings seen in our countryside, from hard gritstones and granites through to the softer limestones, slates and shales. All were used to construct the buildings that harmonize perfectly with our rural landscape. For new builds in many parts of the countryside and especially in the National Parks, local stone will still be used as a facing over a shell built from more modern materials, keeping the building traditions alive today.

## BRICK

Brick-making first came to this country with the Romans. Examples of early bricks and tiles can be seen in the walls at York and other Roman sites around the country.

*Throwley Barn was built slightly later than Throwley Old Hall, but using the same limestone. It is a fine example of an early Tudor long barn.*

*This farmhouse at Scropton, south Derbyshire, has an oak box timber frame with an infill of brick noggin. The roof would originally have been of thatch, but has been replaced with a covering of Staffordshire blue tiles.*

*This photograph illustrates the very decorative estate houses found at Ilam in Staffordshire. They feature elaborate bargeboards with finials and fancy shaped tiles are used to cover the roofs. The same patterns have been repeated on the walls with the art of tile hanging. The stone walls and chimney stacks have decorative embellishments added, all to reflect the estate owner's wealth and importance.*

*This photograph shows the decorative diaper work with diamond patterns on the upper floor and chequer patterns to the lower. It has been created using blue header bricks in the walls of this cottage in Sudbury. Diaper work is a prominent feature of all the estate properties of this south Derbyshire village.*

A revival of brick-making started in the eastern counties of England during the later thirteenth and early fourteenth centuries. This was due to a lack of local building stone, aggravated by timber also now being in short supply. In the country as well as in the towns, brick kilns or clamps were constructed and by the Tudor period brick-making had become a common skill. Good quality brick was now a serious rival to stone, especially with its strong properties when bonded together. In the country, bricks were first made on site using turf-fired clamps and later in brick-built kilns. Not all bricks would be fired to the same standard. The overfired (darker) bricks would be used where they could not be seen as much.

Bricks that had burned to a dark purple or slate colour were often laid using headers to form diamond and chequer patterns. This decorative use of sub-standard bricks became known as diaper work and would be used in the country house down to the humble estate workers' cottages.

Facing bricks are still the most common building material today. Modern bricks, however, are now mass-produced in giant oil-fired tunnel kilns and lack the rustic qualities of their handmade predecessors.

## TILES

Handmade tiles, although used mainly as a roofing material, were also used to cover walls. They were originally found as a feature of buildings in the south-east of England and East Anglia. This protective and decorative finish was revived during the Arts and Crafts period of 1860–1910 and is still a contemporary style today. Handmade clay tiles sometimes shaped on the bottom edge would be hung off wooden laths, a process simply known as tile hanging. In parts of the country where slate was abundant, this would be used in the same way.

## RENDER

Render was used as a finish rather than a structural building material. Its purpose was both as a protection and decoration. The early renders were no more than clays, straw and animal dung.

Later, lime plaster and cement would be used, applied onto a light framework of horizontal strips of wood known as laths. In certain parts of the country, this lime plasterwork would have raised or combed patterns put into it. Pargetting was a common decoration found mainly in Suffolk. Colour was added to the plaster mix to produce pastel shades of pink, ochre and dark reds. In the eighteenth and nineteenth centuries blues and greens were introduced.

A smooth version of plaster rendering became a popular finish about the same time. It was used either totally flat, or sometimes with a fine mortar line chased in just for decoration. This finish originated in Italy and was known as stucco. It lasted as a fashionable finish into the Arts and Crafts period.

ABOVE: *The elaborate diaper patterns form the decorative facings to the walls of Sudbury Hall, south Derbyshire.*

BELOW: *A substantial two-storey farmhouse built in 1610. The red colour to the rendered lime-washed walls was created by adding berries as a dye. It is thought that the reason for the bright colouring was to protect the house against evil spirits. The farmhouse has a typical long-straw thatch, with an extension in the form of a barn for livestock. It has been rebuilt at St Fagans National History Museum.*

Again, the stucco would be painted pastel colours or whitewashed. Another finish used was pebble dash, a rough aggregate of pebbles mixed with cement to give a much tougher result. Paint or whitewash was added to create the final effect.

## BUILDING MATERIALS: ROOFING

We will now turn our attention to the roofs of buildings.

### THATCH

The first material used to put a roof on buildings to keep the weather out would have been some kind of locally sourced thatch. Straw and reed were the most common, although in certain moorland areas bracken and heather were used. Different styles using straw and reed identified a particular region. Thatch continued to be used for vernacular buildings until replacement materials became available, although in some areas of the English countryside, especially Somerset, Dorset and Devon, thatched roofs have been retained. Good thatch lasts for around thirty years and provides a very warm and waterproof cap for cottages and farm buildings. Thatchers have also introduced distinctive trademarks in their work, including patterning and ridge decoration.

However, there are negatives to thatch. It needs regular maintenance and complete replacement from time to time when it has reached the end of its practical use. Also, thatch is a combustible material, making it a problem regarding fires. Another issue is the opportunity for wildlife to set up home within the thatch, which is why thatch today has a protective wire netting covering so as to avoid this happening. For all the negatives, thatch still has the appeal of the traditional image we all associate with the idyllic country cottage, although practical and economic priorities would see some of the cottages and farm buildings have their original thatches replaced with more modern and low-maintenance materials.

*A Devonshire thatched long house, which was common to this area of Devon. This example stands at High Venton, on Dartmoor.*

ABOVE: *This estate cottage in Osmaston village, near Ashbourne, Derbyshire, shows elaborate finishing touches; note the chimneys and fancy bargeboards. The thatched roof is finished with a decorative ridge. Although the cottage looks old, this would have been a revival style used by the estate owners to create effect.*

BELOW: *Devonshire thatched cottages around the village green at Lustleigh. Note the eyebrows to the upper floor windows.*

*This half-timbered cottage at Coton in the Clay, Staffordshire, features large eyebrows to the thatch over the upper floor windows. Note the growth of green moss on the roof. This thatch is definitely in need of replacement.*

## STONE

Where stone was readily available it would be selected and cut to large or small tiles or flags. These were then put onto laths supported on rafters and the roof trusses underneath. The common technique was to put the larger stone flags and tiles on first along the line of the eaves. Then the size would be reduced as they approached the ridge. This material lasted well, with only a minimum of maintenance required.

Plenty of examples of this type of roofing remain today. It is most common in the north-western

*An interesting combination of stone and half-timbered cottages in Broadway, in the Cotswolds – both styles have been capped with a roof of thatch.*

*This row of brick-built cottages in Rolleston-on-Dove, Staffordshire, shows the rectangular style of finish around the upper floor dormer windows.*

counties and those along the Pennines, from Derbyshire in the south to Northumberland in the north. Other areas to use stone in this way were the Cotswolds and counties of central England, from Gloucestershire in the west to Rutland in the east. Wales and Scotland also saw their fair share of stone

roofing wherever the natural material was available. The only disadvantage to stone as a roof covering was the weight, which would affect the roof timbers and cause them to sag. Evidence of this is a common feature of the rural scene.

*Yorkshire gritstone has been used for the walls and for the roof of this farm outbuilding in Stanbury, West Yorkshire. Note the decreasing sizes of stone tiles, from the eaves to the ridge.*

*Local stone has been used to tile the roof of this cottage in Bakewell, Derbyshire. The stones have been put on in different sizes, with the larger ones along the eaves up to the smaller ones at the ridge.*

*A rustic look to this stone-tiled roof on an outbuilding in Hay-on-Wye, on the Welsh/English border. Also worth noting is the weathering to roof, walls, door and window.*

*Large slabs of Derbyshire gritstone are used on this farm building's roof in Beeley, Derbyshire.*

*A close-up of the slate roof of the Hendre-wen Barn at St Fagans National History Museum. Note the thickness and rough cut edges to each slate. Also how the slates are different sizes; again, the smaller ones have been used towards the ridge.*

*The slates on this outbuilding in Cromford, Derbyshire, are very thin, cleanly cut and are all of a uniformed size.*

## SLATE

In the areas of Britain where slate was found, it was used as a building material for both the walls and the roof. The geological properties of slate make it easy to be split into blocks and then split further into sheets. The commercial value of slate was soon noticed and as a result large areas of North Wales, Cornwall and Cumbria were transformed by extensive quarrying. By the nineteenth century, slate quarrying had become a major industry. With the coming of the railways the slate could be transported to all parts of the land, as well as being exported abroad from ports set up just for this purpose.

*This byre has been built using locally sourced large mountain boulders. The roof is constructed from slate, again using decreasing sizes from the eaves to the ridge. This rebuilt example can be found at St Fagans National History Museum.*

*Gritstone has been used for the walls of these two-storey mill workers' cottages. This row features stone mullions and a uniformed slate roof, at Caudwell's Mill, Rowsley, Derbyshire.*

Slate would make an appearance on our rural buildings as a replacement for thatch and other local materials, although the expense saw it originally used only on the more valuable properties. Later, it would be used for the growing towns and cities – with the coming of the Industrial Revolution, slate was used to roof the mills, factories, warehousing as well as housing. It was said that the slate produced from the quarries of North Wales roofed the world!

## TILES

Clay tiles were introduced by the Romans into this country along with bricks. The Roman villas and forts would be roofed using handmade pantiles. After the Roman occupation, tile production completely ceased. Not until 1212 did we see the use of tiles again as a roofing material. This was due to King John, who had issued a building law to replace the thatch in London with clay tiles. At about the same

time, the Archbishop of Canterbury issued a ban on thatch near to the cathedral. This gave rise to the production of tiles again, starting in London and the south-eastern counties. The popularity of brick also saw tiles made in local kilns using local clays and marls dug from pits nearby. Different shades could be achieved depending on the clay used and how it was fired – ochre, orange, reds, browns, blues and even purple colours could be produced. Staffordshire became the centre for this industry, with the Staffordshire blue tiles becoming a common roofing material in central England.

From the fifteenth century, pantiles made their way into this country from the Low Countries of Europe. The Flemish tiles had a distinctive 'S' profile to them, which made them easy to lock together and gave a watertight result. This style of roofing can be seen in North Yorkshire, Lincolnshire, Norfolk, Suffolk and parts of Somerset. Special tiles could

This large limestone-built cottage in Ilam, Staffordshire, is capped with a roof covering of Staffordshire blue tiles.

A brick-built cottage with handmade terracotta tiles. This example was found in Doveridge, South Derbyshire.

The roof of this farm outbuilding has been covered with terracotta pantiles. The distinctive 'S'-shaped profiled tile is common in the north-east of England, Norfolk, Suffolk and parts of Somerset. Culross in Scotland is also famous for its pantile roofs.

be made to fit over ridges and into valleys. Ridge tiles could also be decorated with finials at the ends of gables. However, these embellishments were reserved for estate cottages and buildings, where the visual effect of the tiles and the status of the landlord were foremost.

## OTHER ROOFING MATERIALS

From the late nineteenth century sheet material could be rolled. Corrugated iron became a cheaper and quicker way to roof a building. It was used mainly as a replacement or to patch up thatch and other materials that had seen their best. Corrugated iron was an ideal material for the farmyard. Prefabricated barrelled roofed barns became a common feature. Later, corrugated and sheet asbestos became popular, ideal again for prefabricated buildings, although unfortunately at the time the dangers of this material were unknown.

Roofing felt was, and still is, used to protect many outbuildings on our farms. The felt would be coated with pitch to waterproof it. Lead, copper and zinc were used on the grander manor houses and properties belonging to the estates.

*This large barn on a Dartmoor farm has been fitted with a corrugated metal roof. This material has been used extensively throughout the country to replace thatch on farm buildings. Corrugated metal is also used to cover the roofs of smaller farm outbuildings.*

*From the mid-twentieth century a new material was being used for roofing. This simple prefabricated farm outbuilding has a roof consisting of corrugated asbestos sheeting.*

# WINDOWS AND DOORS

Early windows were just open slits with crude wooden frames, but from the mediaeval to the Tudor period vertically divided mullion frames became the norm. The later period saw the introduction of glass, although this new material was expensive and therefore a luxury. Small panes were held together with frames of lead and were known as leaded lights.

With the introduction of glass, however, there was a need for ventilation. To achieve this, one of the frames would be hinged to open and was called a casement. Mullion windows remained the norm and continued to be used in rural buildings.

In the 1670s, a new solution to the opening window came into this country from France. This style became very fashionable as well as being practical. The new sash windows were made up of two vertical overlapping frames. The glazing area was divided up using thin glazing bars, holding the panes of glass together. The two overlapping frames were fixed into the outer sash boxes, where a system of cords and pulleys would allow one frame to glide over the other, varying the opening position. This type of window, however, was only available to a select few, firstly the gentry in country houses and later the larger farmhouses. It took some time before sash windows were to be seen in the small workers' cottages, the only exception being properties belonging to big estates.

One significant change regarding the amount and layout of windows on a property came about as a result of the imposition of the window tax. This notorious tax was imposed on houses with over a certain number of glazed lights. It was introduced in 1695 when an excise duty was levied on glass and lasted until 1851. Many window openings were filled in to avoid paying this extra tax.

Generally, casement windows were still the preferred style for most rural buildings, with the larger style with one or two opening lights becoming more popular. This style of casement window also saw the introduction of horizontal opening lights and later a combination of both the vertical and horizontal. This style would supersede the sash, becoming very fashionable in the 1920s and 1930s. The top lights were sometimes leaded with pictorial patterns made up from coloured glass.

The most significant change to windows in recent years has been the introduction of double and triple glazing, combined with uPVC frames. The modern way in which we live has resulted in a strong desire

*This barn at Throwley Hall has the early Tudor style of stone mullion frames to the windows. These would be fitted with leaded lights later. The barn, however, has not been fitted with any glass. Also note where some of the windows have been filled in, so as to avoid paying extra window tax.*

*A twelve-pane window, with a sliding opening light, has been used in this small lead miner's cottage in Carsington, Derbyshire. Also of interest is the use of vertical boarded wooden shutters to all the ground floor windows.*

*These stone cottages at Blackbrook, Derbyshire, have sash windows fitted with four panes only, two to each sash.*

*This farmhouse has been fitted with ornate cast metal frames using multiple panes. One or sometimes two sections were hinged to open for ventilation.*

*This picture shows a lead miner's cottage in Wirksworth, Derbyshire. Multiple panes have been used, totalling sixteen in all, with eight to each sash. This style was introduced in the Georgian period.*

*An interesting planked door with slit vents, with a sliding shutter fitted to the inside. As can be seen in this photograph, the shutter has been slid across into the shut position. Note also the extensive weathering to this door.*

for comfort, at the same time achieving energy-saving results. This has convinced most of us to make full use of these low-maintenance materials, even in the countryside, although, in the more sensitive areas, the local authorities have insisted on a more sympathetic use. In most cases, this involves using hard wood rather than uPVC and replacing old frames with perfect reproductions, keeping alive the traditions and character to our rural buildings.

Before we leave the subject of windows, mention must be made of dormers. Most cottages and some farmhouses would use the roof space for upstairs rooms. These rooms would require ventilation and light, so the windows supplied for these rooms would be fitted with the roof wrapping around them. Dormer windows varied in style, with mullions, sashes and casements all being used.

## DOORS AND SHUTTERS

The early window apertures, before glass became readily available, required some way of closing them off in adverse weather. The solution to this was by adding shutters; the wooden-boarded shutters on

A very early Tudor style of boarded door fitted to Hopkinson's House, a former lead merchant's house in Wirksworth, Derbyshire.

Various sizes of doors are seen in this photograph of a gable end to a brick-built barn in Sudbury, South Derbyshire. The larger one at the higher level is the hayloft door. The hay would be dropped from this to the ground or into carts waiting underneath. The smaller lower doors are possibly used to push the hay through to feed the animals inside.

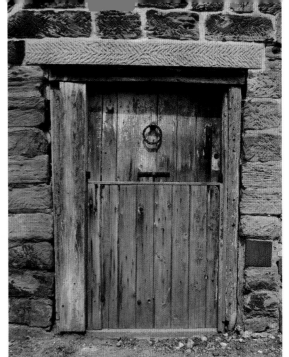

A low-boarded stable door has been fitted to this nail workshop in Belper, Derbyshire. This type of door was common to a building where a forge would have been included. The top half would be opened to give plenty of ventilation from the intense heat, while the bottom half remained shut.

Stable doors feature in this limestone barn in Beeley, Derbyshire, clearly showing the style of hinges and latches used.

the inside of the window frame would slide across to close. However, with the availability of glass to glaze the aperture there was no longer any need for them, although the larger farmhouses and country houses retained shutters as a decorative feature to the interior of a room.

Doors in rural cottages, farmhouses and the early country houses were made up of vertical wooden planking, supported by two or three horizontal battens across the inside. In early examples of this type of door, three or four vertical boards were used; later, six or more planks of oak would be favoured.

By the late seventeenth century panelled doors had become fashionable for those who could afford them. In the country, this new fashion would only be seen on the more affluent properties. The six-panelled door became a distinctive feature of the Georgian period. Four, six and even eight panels were common in the later Regency. By the Victorian age, doors of only four panels became standard. Of course, with constant wear and tear, as well as changes in fashion, doors would be replaced over time.

*This illustrates the detail to a door latch on a farm outbuilding.*

## DOOR FURNITURE

Before we leave the subject of doors it is worth mentioning door furniture. The early planked doors were fitted with long strap hinges and were originally fabricated by the village blacksmith. One end was bent around to fit over a pin fixed to the door frame. Later, this type of hinge would be factory made.

*The stable door to the nail shop in close-up, so as to illustrate the door furniture.*

*This photograph shows the detail of a strap hinge used on a barn door. This was the most common type of hinge to be found on most rural buildings.*

*This illustrates the inside of a stable or barn door and will serve as a useful reference when modelling a door in an open position. Note the arrangement of cross-pieces or battens of the frame.*

The panelled doors had sets of hinges screwed to rebates in the door and in the frame. This arrangement is used today and has become the standard way to hang a door. Other fittings included strengthening straps and studs. These were common on the early planked doors, especially during the Tudor period.

To open and shut doors, a latch would be required. Early examples could be made of wood, with metal styles succeeding them. The panelled door would require a handle or knob fitted as an opening device. Letterboxes and door knockers would also feature as part of the door furniture, as well as numbers to identify the property.

## ROOFLINES AND CHIMNEYS

To conclude our overview, we need to take a look at the details above the height of the eaves. We

*Impressive chimney stacks are seen here in the roof of Ilam Hall, north Staffordshire. Note the curved stone cornice around the top of the stacks, also the chimney pots with their side vents and round petal-shaped crown decorations.*

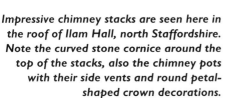

*This interesting roofline photograph shows handmade clay terracotta tiles with fancy curved ridge tiles in the same material. The brick chimney stack has a stone cornice to give a decorative top to the stack. However, only a plain round terracotta pot has been fitted.*

*This photograph illustrates the decorative prominent brick stacks used on estate properties of Sudbury Hall, south Derbyshire. This example features star-shaped caps; all this elaborate work was to show off the landowner's wealth.*

will start by having a look at the chimneys, which are both a functional and integral part of any older house. We mentioned earlier the gap in the ridge of the roof; this was to allow the smoke to escape from a central fire. Later, the need for a flue was required in a purpose-built chimney stack to carry the smoke away. Chimneys became a dominant feature of all houses from the small cottage to the large country house. Construction of the stacks varied depending on the materials used. With the introduction of brick, elaborate and decorative structures appeared. The very decorative chimneys of the Tudor period became a status symbol. Fine examples were commissioned to rise high above the building's roofline, making them impossible to miss.

The familiar chimney pot originated with the Romans and there is archaeological evidence of them being used on mediaeval houses. However, it was not until the Georgian period that the chimney pot became a common feature to the top of the stack. With the move from burning wood to using coal, new designs for fireplaces were required with narrower and separate flues. The pot's purpose was to create more updraught to the narrow flues.

Original chimney pots were thrown by hand on a potter's wheel. After firing they would appear buff or red in colour, depending on the clay used, and would remain unglazed. During the Victorian era, chimney pots would be fabricated using moulds. Square pots started to appear, some with louvres and horns to assist and increase updraught. The moulding process would also allow more elaborate and decorative designs to be produced. Fancy crowns were very popular, as well as ornamental work replicating some of the grand stone and brick Tudor examples. Other additions to the pots came in the form of hoods to keep out the rain. Cowls were also used to direct the smoke away in a desired direction. Recent years have seen a decline in the use of chimney pots, due to the modern forms of central heating used to heat our homes. However, pots are still used as a decoration feature rather than being totally functional.

## BARGEBOARDS

On certain buildings some sort of protection was required to finish the gable ends and dormers. A wooden board was used for this purpose. These are known as bargeboards; some were plain, but others, especially on estate properties, would be very

*Ornate chamfered bargeboards are used to finish this gable to a porch.*

*A combination of gables dressed with bargeboards on these estate cottages at Beeley, Derbyshire.*

ABOVE: *This gable end to a stable block has bargeboards in a scalloped shape, together with fretted cut-outs. The apex is finished with an ornate finial.*

BELOW: *The scalloped design of bargeboards is seen again to decorate the gable of this estate lodge.*

decorative. The boards would have scalloped edges finished with chamfers. Fretted cut-outs were also popular and the apex was often finished with a finial.

## RIDGE TILES AND OTHER CERAMIC ROOFWARE

The ridge of most tiled and slated roofs requires a waterproof cover. Angled or half-round tiles were often used for this, cemented to the roof. Some tiles were finished with a decorative top, although these fancy finishes were usually reserved for the estate properties. The end of the ridge on gables and dormers would have a special tile with a ceramic finial moulded onto them.

*The roofline to this porch is finished with a terracotta finial. These were used as decoration pieces and were fitted to the end ridge tile.*

*This interesting photograph of Ilam Lodge House shows the elaborate use of both bargeboards and decorative facia boarding in the form of a diamond pattern.*

## FLASHINGS

Another way of creating a waterproof join on a roof was by employing lead flashings, used over the ridge, in the valley, or to create a join for a porch or extension roof to a wall. Lead flashing was also used to create the join where a chimney stack would pass through the roof.

## GUTTERINGS AND DOWNPIPES

Early buildings with a thatched roof did not require any guttering at all. The large overhang of the thatching allowed the rainwater to run off clear of the walls

*A very ornate and decorative downpipe and hopper can be seen fitted to the stable block of Sudbury Hall, Derbyshire.*

*Both the guttering and downpipe arrangement are illustrated at a junction of rooflines on this estate cottage at Beeley, Derbyshire.*

*This photograph shows the disc style of wall tie-bar plate used.*

*This photograph is of interest as it shows the guttering and downpipes to this farm outbuilding, together with an uneven line to the roof tiles and a tie-bar plate fitted to the bulging wall in the shape of an 'X'.*

and away. Some farm buildings also did not require guttering. The first purpose-made guttering and downpipes used lead, although after the Industrial Revolution cast iron became the main material for both. The early guttering lengths and the downpipes had a square profile. Later, the half-round profile with round pipes was more commonly used.

At junctions and rainheads the pipes were fitted with hoppers to direct the water. These again were made from lead originally, although cast-iron versions soon replaced them. The larger hoppers used on estate properties would be decorated, sometimes with the heraldic symbols or the coat of arms of the landowner. Cast-iron roof drainage ware started to be produced in mass quantities, but cast iron is brittle and susceptible to damage. Today, most of this has been replaced using modern materials replicating the original profiles where required.

This now concludes our overview of the styles, construction methods and materials used over time in the British countryside. With this knowledge, we can now move on in the next few chapters to describe how to construct miniature versions of some of our rural buildings.

*Another design of tie-bar plate, this time finished in the form of a letter 'S'.*

# CHAPTER TWO

# MAKING A START – RESEARCH, MEASUREMENTS, PHOTOGRAPHY AND WORKING DRAWINGS

## MAKING A START

Over the next few chapters, with the assistance of photographs and illustrations, this book will describe in detail how to create convincing models of rural buildings. A stage by stage process will be followed, with reference to all the materials and techniques used. This way, even a beginner will be able to achieve reasonable results. The scratch buildings shown below are constructed from inexpensive materials, including scrap card and packaging. The methods and materials used here will not cost much in the pocket, but will cost in time. Patience is essential if you are intending to achieve realistic results.

Before you start to build anything, it will first be necessary to carry out a fair amount of research. This will definitely apply to scratch building, but also

to improving kits or off-the-shelf models. We will start with scratch-built models.

## PLANNING FOR SCRATCH BUILDING AND RESEARCH

The first thing to consider is whether you are going to work from a prototype, that is, a model of an existing building. Alternatively, you might want to construct a building that no longer exists, but which fits into the desired location of your layout. It might be that you only want to model part of an existing building, or something freelance but based on a prototype. Whatever your intentions may be, a certain amount of research will be required before you can build a model of it. We will start with building a model of an existing prototype.

*This limestone Cumbrian field barn was picked out for a model to be made for my first DVD (see 'List of Suppliers'). The landowner was contacted so that a survey could be made at the site to gather together all the information required to make a miniature version of the building.*

## A FIELD STUDY

Site visits are essential to obtain the necessary reference required if your building is still standing.

It is worth spending a little time planning how you are going to carry this out. Find out as much information as possible about the building's history and who its current owner is. You will certainly need to obtain their permission before carrying out a survey. Most owners will be happy for you to do this, so long as you make it clear that you only want the information to build a model. It could look rather suspicious to any owner unless you clarify just what your intentions are. However, they will probably insist that any research undertaken on their property is carried out entirely at your own risk.

## TAKING MEASUREMENTS

Once permission has been sought and granted, you can go ahead and organize a site visit. You will need to obtain some equipment for the survey. First, a long tape measure will be required; this will be used to take all the length measurements. A shorter tape is handy to have for measuring windows, doors and other features. For taking the longer measurements it would be a good idea to take a partner along to hold the tape at one end. Second, you will have to measure the height of your building. Heights can

be a more difficult prospect and one way to tackle this problem is by making a height-sighting pole, for example using a metal extendable line prop. Mark off the measurements by wrapping fluorescent or brightly coloured tape around the pole and extend one end to make a flag. You will definitely require the assistance of a partner to hold the pole in position for you. Instruct your partner to stand up close against the wall of the building, then stand a reasonable distance away and take a photograph of both. Estimates of heights can then be made based on this information.

Another way of taking heights, if the building is made from regular-sized blocks of stone or brick, is to measure one block, including the mortar, then count the courses. Some measurements are going to be difficult or impossible to record because of their position. Chimneys and other roofline details, for example, can prove very difficult. These will have to be estimated by gauging them against other features that can be measured, such as the doors and windows.

One other thing to consider is how to determine the pitch or angle of the roof on a gable end wall or dormers. A simple way to obtain this information is by using a folding ruler. These rules are made of metal or wood and are available from most DIY stores or tool shops. To use this method, first position yourself about twice the distance away from the

*The height-sighting pole being held up against the wall of a barn. By taking a photograph of the pole in position, the height can then be estimated.*

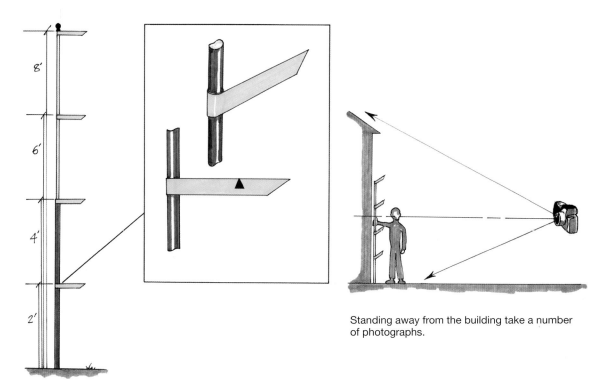

Standing away from the building take a number of photographs.

ABOVE: *This diagram illustrates how a height-sighting pole can be improvised from an extendable line prop. Note how the brightly coloured marker flags have been positioned at significant measurements. The idea is that these will show up on the photographs, making it easy to ascertain the height of the building.*

BELOW: *This diagram explains how the pitch or angle of a roof can be found by using a folding ruler. This method will not be totally accurate, but will be good enough for a model.*

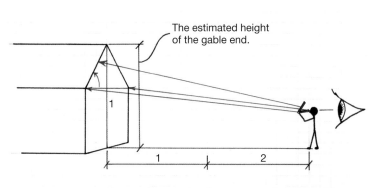

The estimated height of the gable end.

You need to stand a distance away from the gable end. This will be roughly twice the estimated height of the gable end.

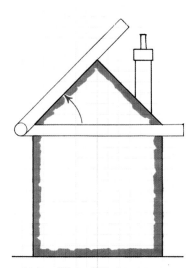

Open up the folded rule to match to angle or pitch of the roof.

gable end wall and lined up with the centre of the triangle shape of the gable end. Hold up the closed rule and line it up level with the two corners, where the roof meets the side walls. Then open up the rule until it matches the angle. Turn it around to make sure the angle matches on both sides. Once you are happy with the match, it is simply a matter of measuring the angle with a protractor in degrees. This method is not totally accurate, but will give a reasonable result that will be good enough for your model.

## A FIELD SKETCH

The next job to be done on site is to produce a field sketch, using a sheet of graph, or any squared, paper on an A4 clipboard. Draw out each elevation using the squares on the paper as a guide. It does not need to be a masterpiece, but try to draw everything in reasonable proportions. When you have drawn your sketch, transfer all the measurements you have taken on to it, including the angles of the roof pitch. Make notes on the sketch of any dominant and interesting features.

The more information you can record at the site, the greater the chance of producing a more accurate and convincing model.

THIS PAGE AND PAGE 46: *A field sketch was produced on the site of the two watermills at St Fagans National History Museum. By producing a sketch like this you can transfer all the measurements you have taken on to it, as well as recording any distinctive features the building might have. This visual document will help you to build an accurate model.*

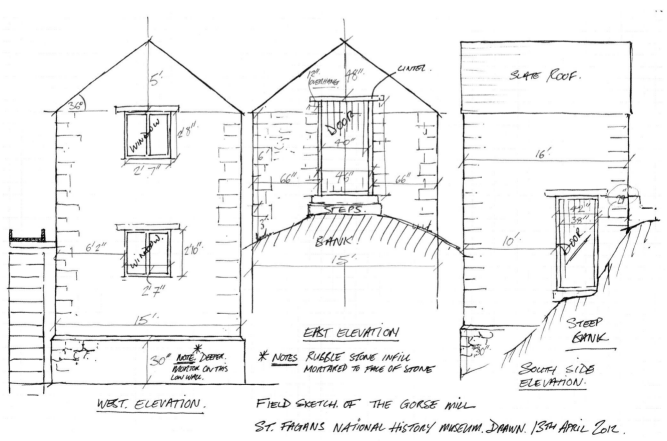

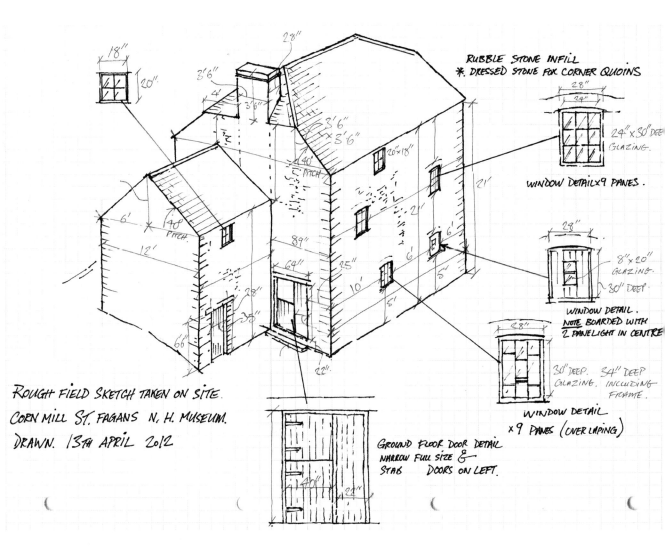

18″
20″

28″

3′6″
4′
3′6″
3′6″
× 3′6″
40″
PITCH

20×18

21′

40″
PITCH

6′
12′

89″

64″

35″

21′

6′

6′

5′

5′

10′

28″

38″

66″

22″

ROUGH FIELD SKETCH TAKEN ON SITE.
CORN MILL ST. FAGANS N. H. MUSEUM.
DRAWN. 13TH APRIL 2012

40″

22″

GROUND FLOOR DOOR DETAIL
NARROW FULL SIZE &
STAB DOORS ON LEFT.

RUBBLE STONE INFILL
✳ DRESSED STONE FOR CORNER QUOINS

28″
24″

24″ × 30″ DEEP
GLAZING.

WINDOW DETAIL × 9 PANES.

28″

8″ × 20″
GLAZING.
30″ DEEP.

WINDOW DETAIL.
NOTE BOARDED WITH
2 PANE LIGHT IN CENTRE

28″

30″ DEEP. 34″ DEEP
GLAZING. INCLUDING
FRAME.

WINDOW DETAIL
× 9 PANES (OVER LAPING)

*A long tape measure will be required to take all the major lengths and widths of the building.*

*A shorter tape measure is useful for measuring the doors, windows and other features.*

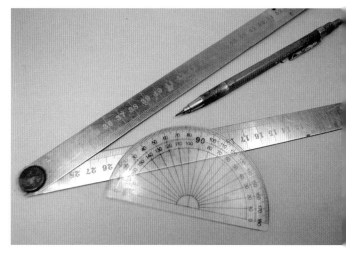

*The other measuring equipment to take on site is a folding metal ruler and a protractor. These are used to calculate the pitch or the sloping angle of the building's roof.*

## FIELD PHOTOGRAPHY

One of the most important items of equipment for your field study will be a camera. A digital camera is strongly recommended, as the convenience and freedom to be able to take lots of pictures of your desired building will be invaluable. Start by taking shots of all the elevations from different angles, then take a series of close-ups. Begin with recording the walls, paying attention to the coursing and corner quoins and window and door reveals. Record the colours and textures of the materials from which the building is constructed.

*A camera, preferably digital, is vital equipment for a site visit and can be used to record buildings from all different angles. The photographs on pages 47–49 are part of a set taken of Gorse Mill at St Fagans National History Museum. Do not forget close-ups of details and any features including colour and weathering references. In fact, record photographically as much as possible, as it will always come in handy for the various stages of building the model.*

Before we move away from the roof, take photographs of the chimney details, as they are a major feature of any roofline. Record the flashings, corbelling around the top, flaunching and of course the chimney pots. The last details to photograph at roof level are the gutterings and drainpipes, including any hoppers and swan necks.

Before you finish on site, do not forget to record the door furniture, such as latches, hinges and so on. If visible, photograph the curtains to the inside of the windows – this can create that special finishing touch to your model.

Keep all your photographs on file and make notes to go with them. They will form extremely valuable reference material. You will need to use them all the time during construction and the final painting and weathering of your model.

## WORKING FROM REFERENCE BOOKS AND OLD PHOTOGRAPHS

There will be situations where for some reason it is not possible to work out in the field. It might be that the building is just too inaccessible to carry out a survey, or in some cases the building no longer exists. If this is the case, you will have to try to find reference photographs, but will undoubtedly have to carry out some extra research to locate such images. Suitable books or collections of photographs may be available, although you will most likely be restricted by the amount of material at your disposal, especially if your desired building was demolished a good number of years ago. Another problem you may encounter is that any photographic image from the past will likely be in black and white, but the model will need to be painted in the correct colours. More research will then be required to determine this information. It might be worth trying to find a building of the same age and from the same area. If you can find something similar, organize a visit to take some colour photographs of it.

The next stage is to ascertain some measurements from which to work. As the actual building cannot be visited, it will be necessary to estimate all

Next, you will need to look at the windows and doors, recording the lintels and sills, as well as the frames themselves. Other ground-level features can also be photographed.

Record the roof covering material, making sure you include the colours and textures and the ways in which the roof has weathered – all valuable information for the finishing stages of your model. Next, look at the other details along the roof, such as the ridges, valleys, flashing details, dormers and chimney stacks. If the building has a thatched roof, record how the thatch overhangs the eaves. Note how it is finished at the ridge and how it wraps around any dormers.

the measurements. One method is to use a piece of tracing paper. Place the sheet over the photograph and pick out a feature such as a door to trace over. (If there is no door visible in the photograph, it will be necessary to find something else of which you have a good idea of its size.) Most doors are around 6ft (1.8m) in height, although some older doors may be only just over 5ft (1.5m). Using this as a guide, move the tracing of the door around the photograph to estimate some of the other measurements. This, of course, will not be totally accurate, but will be good enough for modelling requirements – after all, if the building has long since disappeared who is going to argue that some of your measurements might be a little out!

Other forms of reference might be available that will assist you in your quest. Drawings and plans might exist, although a serious amount of research will be required. Try the Local Planning Office for records of demolished buildings. Another source might be the Local Studies Library. If you are looking for a railway building, try the National Railway Museum's archives at York. The Historical Model Railway Society (HMRS) has a very good collection of photographs and plans in its collection. You would certainly be required to make an appointment with these organizations and you would need to become a member of the HMRS to use its facilities.

*In some cases, it will be necessary to work from photographs and use the tracing-paper method to work out some of the measurements.* Photo: Dave Richards

## PREPARING A WORKING DRAWING

Before you start to construct anything, you will need to prepare a working drawing. All the measurements you have taken will now have to be transferred to the scale at which you are going to build your model. The easiest way to make the conversion is to use a scale rule; these can be obtained from any good modelling tool suppliers. They come in all the popular model railway scales, that is, 2mm, 3mm, 4mm and 7mm.

Drawings can be prepared using a computer if you have the relevant software, or there is always the old-fashioned way of drawing them in pencil or with a fine-line fibre-tipped pen, using a drawing board and a sheet of graph paper. The pre-printed grid on the graph paper will help to keep everything square. Horizontal lines are drawn using the parallel motion on the drawing board or a T-square. All vertical and angled lines can be produced with a set square. For any curves, a compass, circle templates or occasionally French curves are used.

You will need to draw to scale all the elevations of the building , that is, the front, rear and both the end elevations, plus a plan (looking down on the roof). You can also provide a floor plan or footprint for your building, if required. It is always worth adding an extra amount to the height of the wall. This is so as to give the building some footings, allowing the building to sit into the ground surrounding it. Next, the windows, doors and roofline details need to be drawn in position. It might be worth drawing in some of the corner quoins and any half-timbering, if appropriate. The rule is to draw all the major details that you think will help with building the model.

*All my working drawings are prepared on the drawing board. This one was produced for the model of Gorse Mill, using the photographs and field sketch for reference. A working drawing will need to be drawn to the scale of your model.*

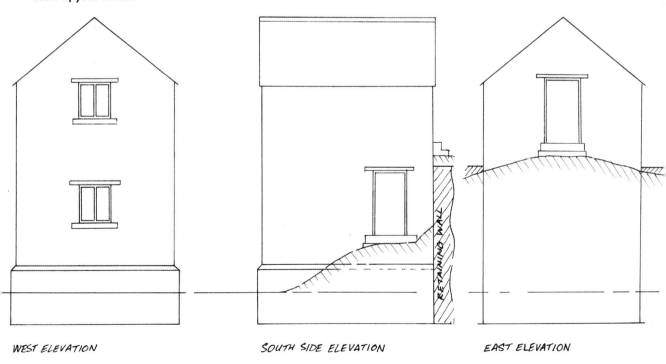

WEST ELEVATION                    SOUTH SIDE ELEVATION                    EAST ELEVATION

DRAWING OF THE GORSE MILL, ST. FAGANS NATIONAL HISTORY MUSEUM.
SCALE = 4 mm ~ 1 FOOT  1 : 76th.

# CHAPTER THREE

# CONSTRUCTING A MODEL

## TRANSFERRING TO THE BUILDING MATERIAL

Now we need to transfer the working drawing over to the material from which we are going to build the model. Foamboard should prove to be an ideal material for most purposes. Foamboard consists of two sheets of card sandwiching a centre core of polystyrene foam. It is not expensive and comes in various sheet sizes and thicknesses of 3mm, 6mm, 9mm and 12mm. It is obtainable from any good arts and craft shop, graphics shops and some of the model suppliers, as well as from some of the larger model railway exhibitions. The 3mm board is recommended for most railway scales; you will find this easier to cut. If a thicker section is required, just double up two or more sheets face to face.

Now you will need to redraw the elevations on to this material. It is a good idea to draw the sides and ends together side by side, as this will make things easier when cutting out. Next, locate all the door and window apertures and draw these in position. One important consideration is to allow for the thickness of the material on all the butt-jointed corners, that is, if the foamboard is 3mm thick, then a total of 6mm will need to be deducted from the length of the front and rear elevations.

## CUTTING OUT THE SHELL

You should now have all the basic components drawn on to the foamboard. The next stage is to cut out everything ready for assembly. The tools required will be a scalpel or hobby knife with a

*This diagram shows the easiest way to draw out the elevations of your building on to the modelling material. Note that the side and end elevations have been put side by side. This makes the task of cutting them out easier. The extra depth to the sides and ends will need to added, to give your building some footings. It is a good idea to cut out the window and door apertures first, before the sides and ends. Do not forget to deduct the thickness of the board from the front and rear elevations.*

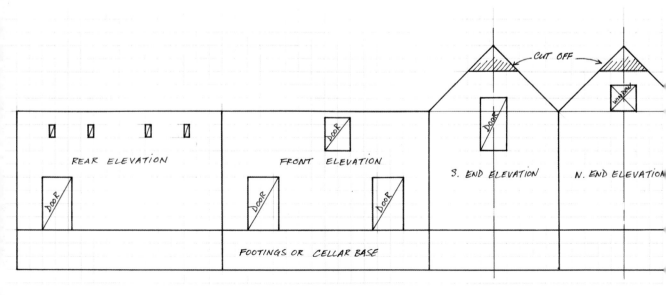

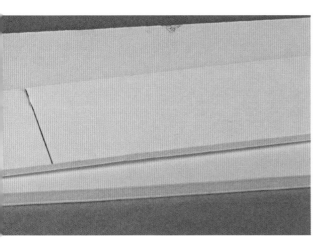

*Foamboard is my preferred material for model building, as it is very light and easy to cut. It comes in a variety of thicknesses, although 3mm is best for modelling.*

sharp blade; a scalpel with a 10A or number 11 blade fitted is ideal. You will need a metal straight edge to cut against; your scale rule can be used for this, but never use a plastic ruler. A cutting mat must be placed underneath the material.

Hold the rule up to your drawn line and guide the tip of the blade on to it. Then with a series of strokes let the knife blade cut into the board. A tip for cutting is to hold the scalpel or hobby knife close up to the blade. This way you will have more control and achieve a cleaner vertical cut. A word of warning when cutting — make sure the straight edge is held firmly down on to the material and that your fingers are not over the cutting edge, otherwise this stage can be rather messy!

Cut out all the window and door apertures first, then all the elevations afterwards. Once you have successfully cut out all the basic wall components, lay them out in order of assembly. Also, save any surplus cut pieces of board as they may come in useful later for bracing.

## ASSEMBLING THE BASIC SHELL

Before starting to glue anything together it is worth considering the adhesives you will be using. For most parts, an ordinary impact adhesive such as Bostik or UHU will be adequate. However, these can attack and dissolve the polystyrene foam used in the foamboard's core. The best solution is to try the adhesive on a piece of scrap board first. If the glue does have an effect, then you must use an alternative adhesive, such as PVA glue, which will bond the foamboard

*When cutting out the foamboard, hold the scalpel or hobby knife close to the blade to ensure a cleaner and more vertical cut. Always cut against a metal rule with a cutting mat underneath; never use a plastic ruler for this purpose.*

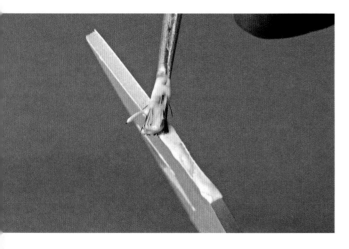

*If gluing across the core of the board always use PVA rather than impact adhesives, which can affect the polystyrene core.*

without affecting the centre core. The slight disadvantage of this adhesive is that it will not bond straight away.

It will be necessary to secure the joint with dressmaker's pins until the glue sets. It is also a good idea to put a small square up to the joint to make sure a right-angled corner is achieved. Once the PVA has set firm, remove the pins. Repeat this exercise on all the corner joints until all four walls are in position.

To make the shell more rigid, add some bracing. Bracing helps to alleviate any warping taking place at later stages when the building's skin has been added. Scraps of foamboard from the cutting-out process are ideal for bracing. For example, the angled pieces cut from the gable end walls can be reused to form corner bracing for the four walls. As always, if gluing across the core of the board, use PVA glue and pin

*This diagram shows how to fix the corner of your building together. You can see the reason for deducting the thickness of the board from the sides when making a butt joint – for example, when working with 3mm thick foamboard, it is necessary to deduct 6mm from the total length of the sides. Corner and lateral bracing using cut-off sections of board is also shown.*

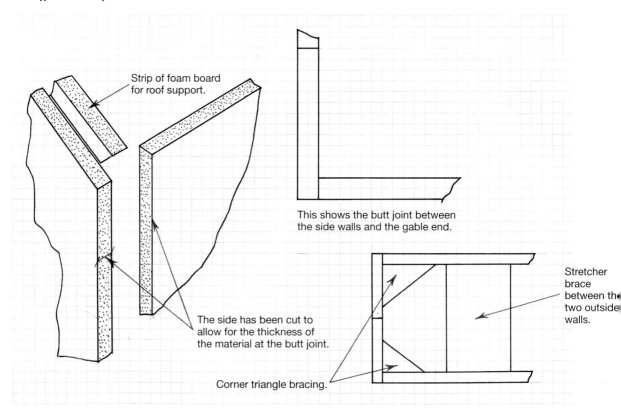

Strip of foam board for roof support.

This shows the butt joint between the side walls and the gable end.

The side has been cut to allow for the thickness of the material at the butt joint.

Stretcher brace between the two outside walls.

Corner triangle bracing.

*When fixing the gable end wall to the side wall, use PVA glue then secure the join with dressmaker's pins until the bond has been made and use a small square to check that the corner is at a right angle.*

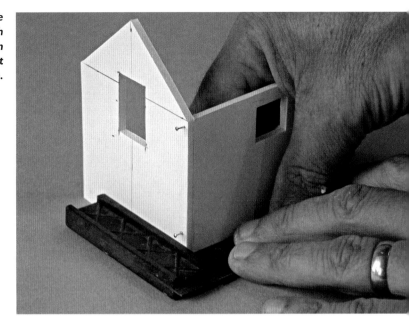

*These are the two main adhesives you will need in the construction of your model buildings. Superglue may be necessary at the later stages to glue on any metal or plastic parts.*

in place until secure. A tip when adding bracing is to avoid putting the pieces too close to a window or door apertures, as this might make fitting them more difficult.

Next, if any extensions are required these will need to be constructed in the same way, before joining them to the main building. Once you are happy with the basic shell and sufficient bracing has been added, you can move on to the next stage of construction.

## ADDING THE SKIN TO THE BUILDING

### STONEWORK

The shell of your building will now require a skin, which will replicate the material of the building's walls. We will start by looking at how to create a model of a building that was made from stone.

DAS air-drying modelling clay is a good material from which to recreate stone. It is a natural clay that comes in a slab sealed in an air-tight packet and is available from any good arts and crafts shops, model shops and from some tool and materials suppliers, as well as being found at exhibitions. As DAS is an

*To produce the skin for the buildings I use DAS, a natural air-drying clay.*

*Always reseal the packet straight after use; a bulldog clip is good for this.*

air-drying clay, the packet must be resealed straight away after use; a bulldog clip is good for this. When not using the clay for a while, it is a good idea to wrap it in a damp cloth and seal it in a polythene bag. This will ensure that it will remain fresh for the next time you need it.

Before applying the clay, you will first need to coat the shell with adhesive – dilute PVA will be fine for this purpose. Brush a light coating of PVA on both the outside and inside of the shell. The reason for coating both sides is to avoid movement – the inside coating will help to counteract any warping.

Next, take a small amount of the clay, certainly no bigger than the size of a large marble, and push it into the PVA on the surface. Spread the clay out using your fingers until you have achieved the desired thickness of the prototype. You will have to gauge this by eye. Once you are happy with the result, it is a matter of repeating this exercise until the building has a skin of the clay all the way round. Make sure that you have gone around the corners of the building and into the apertures. You can apply the clay in stages, as the fresh clay will blend with any drier clay perfectly. Also, more clay can be added to an area if the first attempt was unsuccessful. You must be prepared to be patient with this process – the secret is just to add a little at a time and try not to rush it.

You can now put your model away for a while as the clay will need at least twenty-four hours to completely dry off. Once the skin has dried to a chalk-like surface, it will be ready for you to move on to the next stage of construction.

*When applying clay to the shell of the building, first coat the shell with dilute PVA. Then push a small amount at a time on to the surface and spread using your fingers until it is the desired thickness of the material you are trying to replicate.*

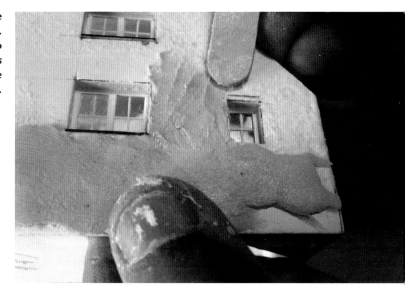

## SCRIBING OUT THE STONEWORK

This is another stage that will require a considerable amount of patience and dedication. Take it slowly and you will be rewarded with encouraging results. Start by drawing a few guidelines. Using a small square up against the corner, draw some parallel lines. Then draw in some vertical lines; these will ensure that your coursing is level. Also draw some of the larger stones such as quoins, lintels and sills.

It might be necessary to clean up around corners and into the apertures. This can be done using a small square or flat file together with some fine sandpaper. You may wish to sand down the face of the clay, especially if your building is constructed from regular-sized dressed stone.

*With the clay skin complete and dry, you can now start to clean up around the window and door apertures and any corners.*

*I use a scalpel with a blunt 10A blade fitted to do all the scribing. An old toothbrush is also used to brush the waste away while scribing.*

The following tools are required for scribing. A Swann-Morton scalpel with a blunt 10A blade fitted will do the job well (a fresh blade is not necessary, so save all your blunt blades for this). An old toothbrush is needed to brush away the debris as you go. A face mask should be worn as the dust created can be irritating.

With the guides drawn and corners cleaned up, you can start to scribe the stonework. Referring to the photographs of the prototype taken at the site, start with the corners, scribing the corner quoins if relevant. Then move on to the lintels and sills of the windows and doors. Follow the guidelines that you have drawn and use a small metal ruler to start with, but when you have you gained confidence you can start scribing in freehand. If you make a mistake, just add some more clay and rescribe when dry.

If your prototype is built from regular stone, continue along the same lines and keep the coursing straight. However, if the building is constructed from irregular or a rubble stone infill, you can be a little more loose with your scribing, but follow the shapes from your photographic reference and remember to keep the coursing level. Don't worry, no one will expect every stone to be in the right position – so long as you create the general effect it

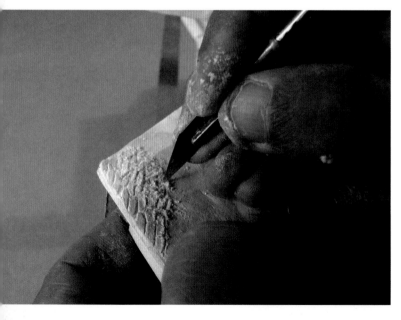

*This photograph shows the process of scribing rubble stone to the gable end of a barn.*

*This picture illustrates using an old toothbrush to brush away the waste clay as you go along. Save the waste powder as it might come in useful for the later stages of your model.*

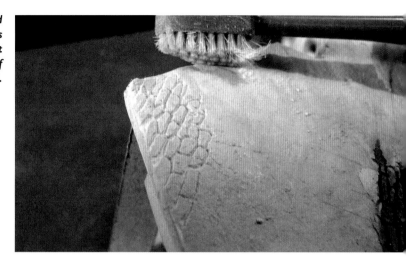

*Pictured are the results of scribing rubble stone on a model limestone barn. Note that although the rubble stone is irregular, the coursing is still kept reasonably level.*

will look correct on your model. The residue dust produced from scribing can be saved and brushed into the gaps to recreate the effect of remortared stone or brickwork.

## SCRIBING BRICK

For brickwork, use the same techniques and equipment as for stone, create the skin using ready-mixed plaster filler. No More Cracks, produced by UniBond, is ideal for the job, as it has a gritty texture that gives it a good representation of facing bricks. This time, the plaster is brushed in a thin coat on to the shell with PVA glue and left to dry off.

It is important to draw in more guidelines for scribing brickwork, making sure the coursing is

*No More Cracks ready-mixed plaster filler is ideal for recreating render. The gritty texture to the mix when brushed on is very authentic. It can also be used for brickwork and other finishes.*

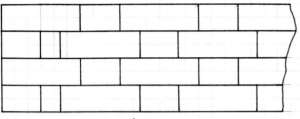

**A**

Flemish Bond – This is double thickness, without a cavity. Found in most rural buildings.

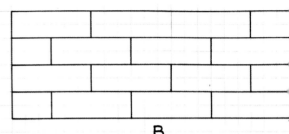

**B**

Stretcher Bond – More common in modern buildings, this is usu as an outer skin with cavity between the inner and outer walls

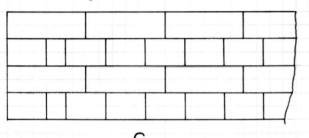

**C**

English Bond – Another non-cavity wall. This bond is also common for buildings in rural areas.

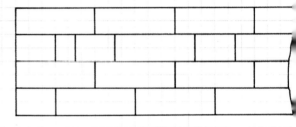

**D**

Flemish – Garden Wall Bond – Used when both the sides of the wall are going to be visible.

*This diagram illustrates the common bonding of bricks found in the British Isles. The brick bonding will vary depending upon the age of the building. Older buildings were built without a cavity. Most of our rural buildings will have the Flemish bond as seen in illustration 'A'.*

all level. Then it is down to scribing all the brick courses to the correct bonding of the prototype. Alternatively, pre-scribed styrene sheet can be used if you find the prospect of scribing it yourself too daunting. However, if you use this material you must be careful to make sure all the corners join up and the coursing following around is correctly lined up.

## RENDER

The No More Cracks plaster mix is also ideal for recreating a rendered finish. Using a brush, apply this material straight from the tub to your building. When it has dried, work on it a little with the tip of the scalpel blade to show the render cracking away to reveal the brick underneath. Such an effect will add more character to your model.

## COB, PLASTER AND FLINT

To reproduce materials such as cob and plaster infills, use the DAS modelling clay again. Apply it to the desired thickness, but this time leave it without any scribing (although a little cracking scribed on will not look out of place). Applying the DAS as an infill of a timber-framed building will be described in one of the projects later in the book.

Flint can be either scribed in rounded patterns into the surface of the DAS, or by blobbing on plaster filler with a brush. The first technique is ideal for the larger scales, but for smaller scales plaster filler is preferable. By using a stencil brush, this can be stippled on to give a reasonable-looking effect. Pargetting patterns such as combing can be reproduced using both the DAS and the plaster, although a great deal of care will be required to achieve the correct results.

## ADDING THE BASE COLOUR

Before carrying on with the construction of the model, it will be necessary to give the shell of the building a base colour of paint. It will be easier to

*The first coat of paint should be applied to the skin of the building, before fixing any windows, doors or the roof. The paint used for this stage will be a wash of oil paint (10 per cent paint to 90 per cent turpentine or thinners). The colour needs to match the mortar or the gaps between the courses of the stone.*

*Capillary action will take the wash of paint into all those gaps, giving an instant result. The paint will also soak into the clay or plaster to give a base for the stone or brickwork. The finished effect of this first coat of paint is shown here.*

apply this now rather than when all the windows and the roof have been fitted

The colour required for this first coat will need to match the mortar or gaps between the courses. Artist's oil paints are a good choice for all the painting stages. The base colour needs to be applied as a wash. Mix 10 per cent paint from the tube to 90 per cent turpentine or thinners in a suitable jar or tin. Using a fairly large brush, apply the wash of paint to the skin of the model. The wash will soak into the clay or plaster and capillary action will carry the colour wash into all the scribed mortar lines. Being so thin, the paint will be touch-dry in seconds.

## WINDOWS AND DOORS

### MATERIALS
The next stage is to make up and fix in position all the windows and the doors. It is easier and more practical to fit them before putting the building's roof on. The materials for windows can be readily obtained – old greetings cards and celluloid or acetate film saved from packaging are ideal. It is preferable to use double-sided adhesive tape for making up the frames – glue can be rather messy as it tends to ooze out on to the face of the glazing material.

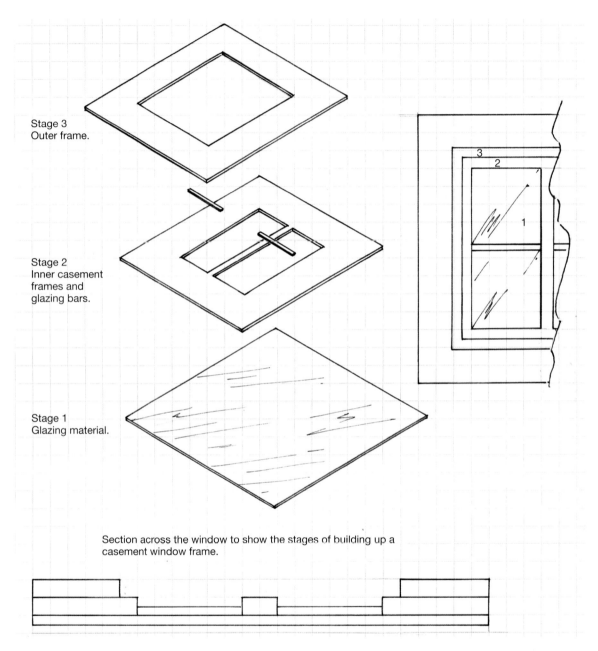

Stage 3
Outer frame.

Stage 2
Inner casement
frames and
glazing bars.

Stage 1
Glazing material.

Section across the window to show the stages of building up a
casement window frame.

*It is important that a casement window is assembled in the correct order, as shown here. Be very careful when cutting out the frames and always use a new blade in your scalpel or hobby knife to achieve the best results.*

Use one of the more expensive brands of adhesive tape; the cheaper ones dry out quickly and lose their tack, which will eventually cause the window frame to fall apart. Doors can be made from card or from pre-grooved styrene sheet.

## MAKING UP THE WINDOWS

Before construction, a drawing will be required. Measure the aperture first, then draw the dimensions on to a sheet of graph paper. Draw the outer frames, then add the inner frames for fixed and

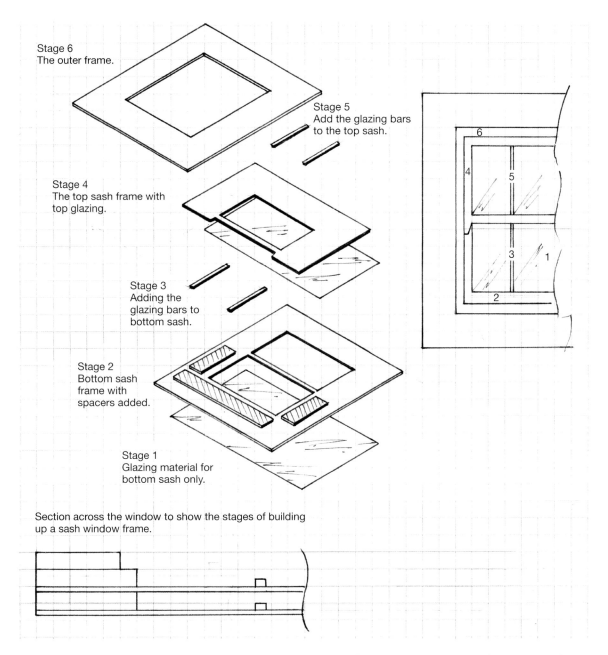

Stage 6
The outer frame.

Stage 5
Add the glazing bars
to the top sash.

Stage 4
The top sash frame with
top glazing.

Stage 3
Adding the
glazing bars to
bottom sash.

Stage 2
Bottom sash
frame with
spacers added.

Stage 1
Glazing material for
bottom sash only.

Section across the window to show the stages of building
up a sash window frame.

*This method should be followed when making up a sash window frame. Note that each sash must be made as a separate unit, which will create an extra layer to the assembly. Also on the top sash a little extra should be added to the frame on each side to create the horns.*

opening casement lights, or top and bottom sash frames. Lastly, draw all the glazing bars in position. You will need to use the drawing as reference and to position the glazing bars.

In order to make up the windows, first select some clear celluloid or acetate film packaging of about 0.25mm thickness. Cut out a section, which should be 10mm larger all the way round than the aperture – check it against your drawing. To make the frames, use selected greetings cards of about the same thickness as the glazing material, that is, 0.25mm thick. Make sure that you have the inside matt or uncoated side of the card facing up. All the drawing and colouring must be done on this side of the card – you will not be able to apply this to the coated side. Now draw the frames on to the card, making sure that all the sizes are correct and allowing for overlaps. Before you cut them out, add the double-sided tape to the rear (coated side of the card), leaving the outer-facing backing in place. Always use a fresh, sharp blade in your scalpel or knife. A number 11 blade is recommended for a scalpel as it will get into the tight corners. Carefully cut out the frame to the inside first. It is important that the frames are cut out and assembled in the correct order.

Next, peel off the backing paper from the double-sided tape and fix the first frame on to the celluloid. The outer frames now need to be fixed on top of the inner frames, leaving a ledge the width of the inner frame showing.

Casement windows are made up from two frame layers. Sash windows, however, require three layers; the top and bottom sashes will overlap like the prototype. The only way to construct these is by making each sash up as a separate unit. On the top sash, the horns on the stiles or sides of the frame need to be included and a packing frame is required in the assembly.

Glazing bars can be cut from adhesive labels, readily available from any stationers. A great amount of care is needed when cutting out such thin bars, so always use a sharp blade and make a series of cuts. If you try to cut through too quickly the thin strip will just coil up like a watch spring. Peel the backing paper away and very carefully position the strip on to the glazing. Use your drawing to guide you into the correct position. With the tip of the blade, nick the surplus paper away, then lightly burnish the strip to join with the card frame. Where glazing bars affix the panes of glass together, the join can be represented by overlapping the paper strip. It will be so that fine the overlap will not be noticed.

If the window frames require colour, it is not advisable to try to paint them. Unless you use the finest of brushes and have the confidence, the chances are that the paint will end up on the glazing as well. It is far better to use marker pens to add the colour. The Promarker range of pens produced by Letraset is ideal for this. With over ninety colours available,

*A four-pane sash window with two panes to each sash. The horns on the upper sash frame can be clearly seen.*

*Some of the range of Promarker pens produced by Letraset. These are ideal for colouring window frames. The ink will soak into the card frames and paper glazing bars, but will be repelled from the glazing material itself, which is much quicker and neater than trying to paint them.*

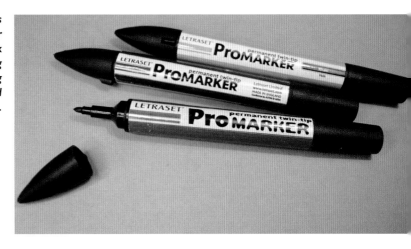

ABOVE: *Here, the inner frames were coloured first, then the outer frame was coloured before it was fixed in position over the inner opening casement frames to give the two-colour paint finish to the window.*

LEFT: *Two windows that have been made up and coloured with Promarker pens before being cut out and fixed into their final position.*

there will be something to match your chosen prototype's shade. The ink from the pens will soak into the card and paper, but be repelled from the glazing material. This provides a much cleaner and quicker way of applying colour to the window frames, giving convincing results without much effort.

## MAKING DOOR FRAMES AND DOORS

Door frames can be easily fabricated from strips of mounting card or balsa wood. Care will be needed to cut the mounting card as it only needs to be a few millimetres wide. Put the strips up to the apertures that have been cut out ready for the doors and mark the heights and widths on the strips.

Now you can look at fitting a door into the frame, following the style of the prototype. A vertical planked door is the most common style to be found in rural buildings. Card of 0.5mm thickness is best for doors and you might be able to find a greetings card or card packaging that can be used for this purpose. Mark out the size of the aperture including the door frame. Then mark out the widths of the planks and draw them in. Then by using the back of the knife blade, score along the pre-drawn lines. Turning the blade over, lightly use the tip of the blade to create a 'V' groove by drawing it along the pre-scored line.

These boarded doors will of course require door furniture. Some of them will be fitted with strap hinges on the outside, while others will have them fitted to the inside on the frames, although the latter

*This diagram shows how to make a vertical planked door out of card. Illustrations (A) and (B) show the style of framework using cross-battens and an extra diagonal batten to give strength to the door; (C) shows how the front-facing planking should appear; (D) shows how to score the planks by using the tip of the scalpel blade to make the 'V' groove.*

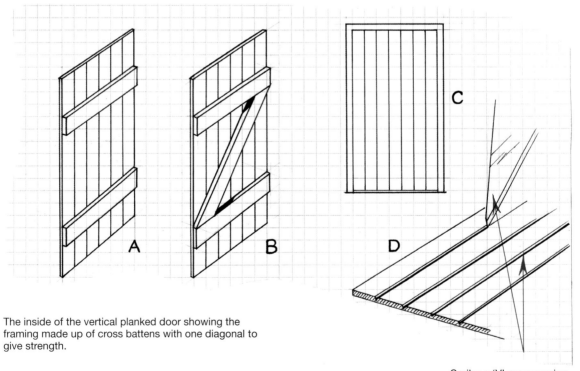

The inside of the vertical planked door showing the framing made up of cross battens with one diagonal to give strength.

Scribe a 'V' groove using the tip of the scalpel blade.

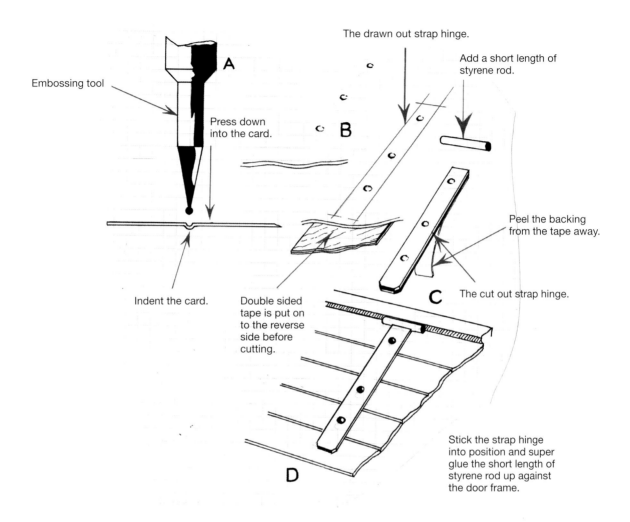

Embossing tool

A

Press down into the card.

Indent the card.

Double sided tape is put on to the reverse side before cutting.

The drawn out strap hinge.

Add a short length of styrene rod.

B

C

Peel the backing from the tape away.

The cut out strap hinge.

D

Stick the strap hinge into position and super glue the short length of styrene rod up against the door frame.

*This diagram shows the making up of a strap hinge. (A) Use an embossing tool to indent the back of the card to produce a bolt head on the front, but do not apply too much pressure so that you go through the card; (B) Add the double-sided tape to the back of the card, in line with the raised bolt heads; (C) Cut out the strap hinge, now by peeling away the backing – the hinge is now ready to be positioned on the door; (D) Superglue a small length of styrene rod added to form the hinge itself.*

will only apply if the door is to be modelled in an open position.

The strap hinges can once again be made from strips of greeting card. The first operation is to fabricate the bolt heads. These need to be marked in position on the coated side of the card. Using an embossing tool, press the ball tip into the material until the impression shows on the other side of the card. Be careful when carrying this out – you will need to apply enough pressure to make the bolt head, but not too much that you puncture the card. Practise first on a scrap piece until you are happy with the results. Next, fix a strip of double-sided tape to the coated (reverse) side, then carefully cut out the strap. You need to cut through both the card and the tape on the back. Now peel off the backing from the tape and position it on to the door. To finish off, the hinge part can be made from a short length of styrene rod superglued to where the strap meets the door frame.

Latch made from a wire staple.

Press-down latch made from wire.

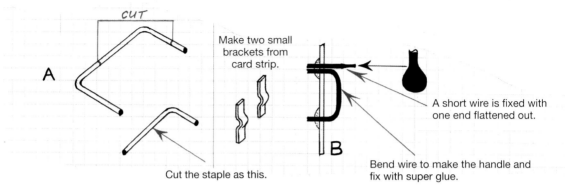

CUT

A

Make two small brackets from card strip.

A short wire is fixed with one end flattened out.

B

Cut the staple as this.

Bend wire to make the handle and fix with super glue.

*The final diagram in this set shows how to make two common styles of door latch used on this type of door. (A) The sliding latch can be made for the larger scales by cutting a small wire staple to size then adding two small strips of card cut down to form the brackets to hold the latch; (B) shows how to make a (press down) opening latch from bending a small length of wire to form the handle and flattening it at one end.*

To complete the planked doors, a door latch will be required. This can be fabricated from wire, but first you need to drill or punch two small holes into the door, then bend a small, fine length of wire through the holes and superglue it to secure. Trim off any wire hanging over at the back when the glue has set. A second small length of wire needs to be flattened out at one end and inserted just above the top hole of the handle to form the latch.

Panelled doors are not so common in rural areas and are only usually found as replacements for boarded planked originals. This type of door can be made again from card by first cutting the backing to size. Then assemble the door frame to the edge, before assembling the panels. The uprights known as stiles and cross-rails can either be cut in strips, or cut out from one piece of card. Use double-sided tape again for assembly rather than glue. Once all your windows and doors have been assembled you can fit them into the apertures of your building. You will need to cut them out or use the overlapping extra material to fix to the inside of the apertures.

*This photograph shows a typical press-down latch. This is the most common type of latch to be found on the doors of rural properties.*

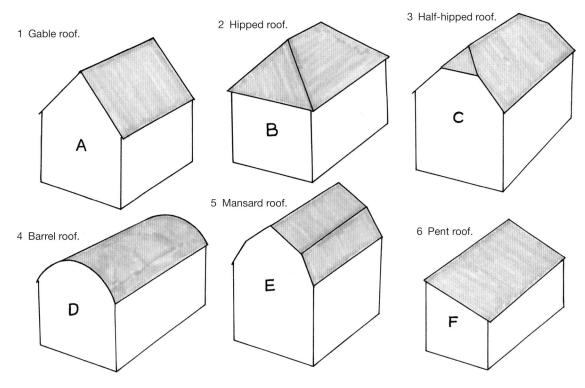

1 Gable roof.

2 Hipped roof.

3 Half-hipped roof.

4 Barrel roof.

5 Mansard roof.

6 Pent roof.

*The main types of roof shapes and profiles to be found in the British Isles.*

## FITTING THE ROOF

Now the windows and doors are all fitted, it is time to look at fitting the roof to your building. There are two main types of roof – gabled and hipped. Variations include half-hipped and double-pitched (mansard) roofs.

The first stage is to fit the sub-base for the roof. This can be made up from different thicknesses of card, or foamboard if you are representing a thatch. To hold up the sub-base of the roof, a support strip will need to be added to the inside of the gable end. In the case of hipped and long gabled roofs a number of truss supports will be required. These can be made from card or foamboard and will need to be let into the walls. It is also recommended to put in a ridge strip to hold the two gable ends together, or between two roof trusses. Two more strips can be inserted at the angle of the roof's pitch; these will represent the purlins and add even more support.

The card sub-base can now be glued into position as a folded tent piece for the gabled roof. Four separate panels are needed to recreate a hipped or half-hipped roof.

Extra work will be required on the sub-base if you are trying the recreate a dip in the ridge or the sagging in an old roof. This feature is common in rural buildings where the timbers have moved over time. Also this adds a rustic character to the building, making it more attractive and interesting. To create this feature in our models, glue formers on to the sub-base, with another top piece of card bent over them. The dip is created by cutting a curve to the ridge top of the card sub-base. Bring the two curved ridge edges together and run a length of masking tape along the ridge to secure. This technique is for sub-bases that will be covered with slates, tiles or sheeting.

The sub-base for a thatch will be constructed in the same way, but using the thicker foamboard.

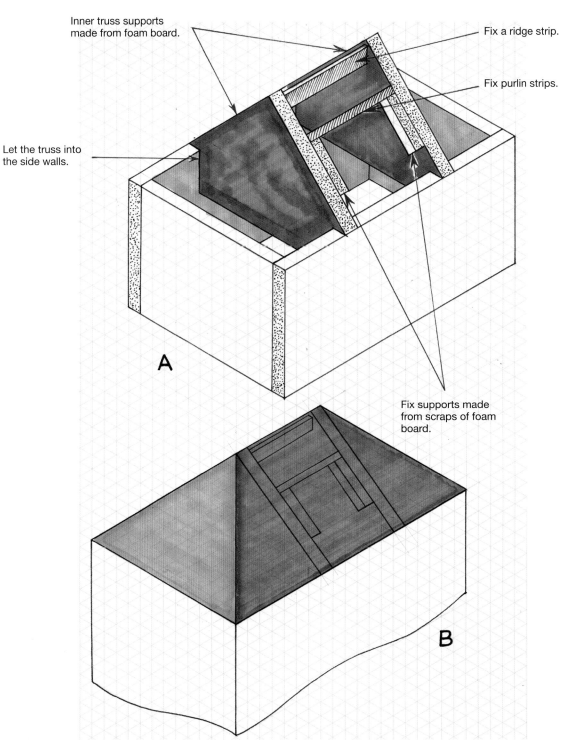

Inner truss supports made from foam board.

Fix a ridge strip.

Fix purlin strips.

Let the truss into the side walls.

A

Fix supports made from scraps of foam board.

B

*This diagram illustrates how to make the truss frame for a hipped or half-hipped roof. The trusses have to be let into the main walls. Note how pieces of scrap board have been utilized to make supports, purlins and the roof ridge strip.*

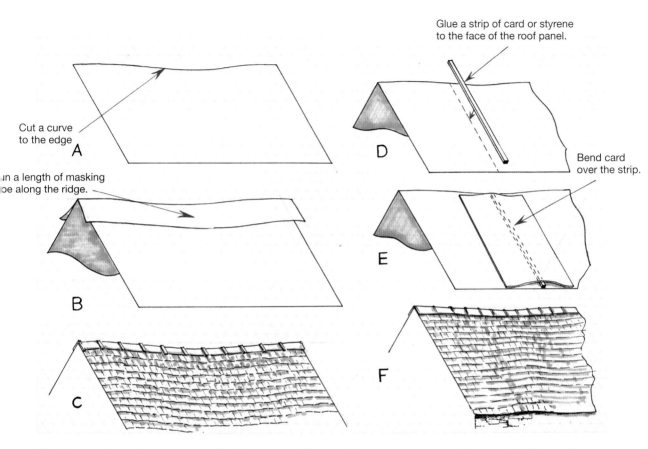

Cut a curve
to the edge
A

...n a length of masking
...e along the ridge.

B

C

Glue a strip of card or styrene
to the face of the roof panel.

D

Bend card
over the strip.

E

F

*This diagram shows how to create the dips, sags and bumps that are common on older rural buildings where the timbers have moved over time. (A) First, cut a slight curve to the edge of the card roof panel; (B) When fixed to the walls and gable ends, run a piece of masking tape along the join to secure its shape at the ridge; (C) The finished result when all the tiles are added will create the dip; (D) The method used to create the bump, where the roof has sagged each side of a truss, requires adding a strip of card to the face of the panel; (E) Bending a thin piece of card over the strip will give the sub-base; (F) The final bump in the tiled roof.*

The thickness of the board needed will depend on the thatch you are trying to replicate and the scale of your model. Before gluing the roof panels into position, you will need to strip off the top sheet of facing card, leaving the polystyrene core exposed. The top ridge can now be curved at an angle, so that the panels meet up when they are brought together. After fixing and gluing the panels into position, the edges can be curved and shaped around any dormers. To finish, the ridge and edges can be rounded off using sandpaper.

## ROOF COVERINGS

This section describes how to make and cover your roof with slates or tiles. The process is the same for both, although the slates will need to be much thinner than tiles in most cases. You will have to judge the thickness of the prototype, replicating this by selecting material of an appropriate thickness, also taking into consideration the scale of your model. If your chosen building is well maintained, the slates/tiles should be cut and placed in uniform rows. However, most rural buildings will be of a certain age, or not so well maintained. In these cases, the

*This photograph taken of a farm outbuilding in Bonsall, Derbyshire, is a good example of a dip or sag to the ridge.*

*Save all your Christmas and other greetings cards to reuse on your models.*

slates/tiles need to be placed individually to create the right effect.

Old Christmas cards are ideal for modelling purposes as they vary in thickness, which will give a realistic effect to your slates and tiles. You will also be doing your bit for recycling by putting them to a creative use. I save all my Christmas cards for my models.

Once you have selected a card of an appropriate thickness, draw a grid on the inside. Mark the width and depth of each slate or tile. The depth needs to include the overlap; it is a good idea to mark the overlap in a different colour, as this will help when you come to position the slates/tiles on to the roof.

When the grid is complete, you can start the cutting out process. We will begin with the well-maintained roof. Starting on the bottom edge of the card, cut with your knife along each slate/tile up to the red overlap line; repeat this exercise along the length of the row. Next, cut along the full length of the row. To add a little variation and realism, cut the corner off at an angle on the odd tile or slate to represent a broken one.

For an unmaintained, rustic-looking roof, cut the slate/tiles along the vertical lines. This will give you a strip only the width of one tile or slate. Now cut them individually along the black line above the overlap. Collect either the strips or individual tiles and slates ready for applying on to the sub-base of the roof.

## APPLYING THE TILES AND SLATES TO THE ROOF

The slates/tiles could be glued to the sub-base of the roof, but this can get rather messy, so double-sided

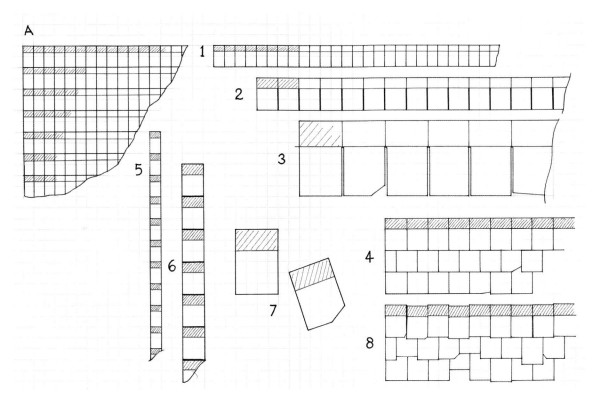

*This diagram illustrates the process for cutting tiles and slates. On well-maintained roofs where the tiles or slates will remain in regimented rows follow stages 1–4, for the more rustic look to a roof found on older properties, follow stages 5–8. The first stage, however, is to mark out the tiles or slates on to your card. (A) The red shaded area indicates where the tiles or slates will overlap on the rows. Start by cutting with the scalpel from the edge up to the red line to represent each tile or slate. Then cut each row along the next black line to create a strip. (For the well-maintained option cut them into horizontal strips, for the rustic cut them into vertical strips.) The strips for the maintained roof can now be assembled on to the sub-base, but before you do this, just take the corner off the odd one to represent a broken tile or slate. For the rustic roof, each slate/tile will need to be cut out separately and then assembled one by one to the sub-base of the roof, just in the same way as on a real roof. Illustrations 4 and 8 show how the finished assembled roof coverings for both versions should appear.*

adhesive tape is once again preferable. Place this on to the sub-base, peel the backing paper away and place the rows or individual tiles in position. The technique is the same for both. Start at the bottom edge or the eaves. This first row will need to over-hang slightly to represent the rain run-off into the guttering or clear of the walls. You may have to use a half-width slate or tile at the end of the row. With the first row complete, move on to the next, remembering to overlap the first row by half in the width and a third in the depth.

Fix the others on in this manner, applying them until you have reached the ridge. If you are fixing individual slates/tiles, avoid making them level with each other along the visible edge of the row. Also cut the corner off the occasional one to represent a broken slate/tile as before. Move one or two even further down on the edge to represent the slipped ones. These touches can be applied to the regular rows as well.

*Instead of gluing the rows or individual tiles and slates to the roof, use a good quality double-sided adhesive tape.* Photo: Dave Richards

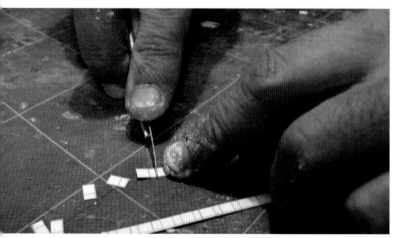

*This illustrates the cutting of the individual slates to roof the model of the Gorse Mill.*
Photo: Dave Richards

*Here the strip of double-sided tape is fixed to the sub-base ready to take the slates.*
Photo: Dave Richards

*The first cut slate is positioned on the first row along the line of the eaves; do not forget that the first row will need to overhang by about one-third to allow the rainwater to run into a gutter or clear of the walls.* Photo: Dave Richards

*The tiles are assembled along the eaves to complete the first row.* Photo: Dave Richards

*Place the second row overlapping to the red line (about one-third). Remember that if you started the first row with a full slate or tile, then the second row must start with a half slate or tile to retain the overlapping pattern.* Photo: Dave Richards

The finished stone flag tiling, fixed to the model barn roof. These were all assembled individually to create this rustic effect. Note the dip in the roof, which has been created using the methods described. A thin coat of plaster filler has also been added, brushed over all the tiles to seal them and to give a stone texture to the surface. This model is in 7mm scale so this detail would be required; in smaller scales it probably would not be noticed. *Photo: Dave Richards*

The sags to the ridge and the bumps along the pitch of the roof are clearly shown here in this model of a Cumbrian field barn. Again on this 7mm model, the stone roofing flags received a coating of the plaster filler.

*Plumber's hemp can be purchased by the hank.*

## CREATING A THATCH

Long straw and reed are the most common materials used for thatching in the United Kingdom; plumber's hemp works very well as a material for reproducing them. You should be able to acquire plumber's hemp from a builder's merchants or specialist plumber's trade supplier, or from a modelling supplier such as Malcolm's Miniatures (*see* List of Suppliers).

The first stage is to cut the plumber's hemp into smaller bundles. Then cut again into even smaller bundles, for example about 15mm in length for 4mm scale. Lay the bundles of hemp out ready to start fixing them to the foamboard sub-base. First, place a

*This illustration shows how thatch is finished around dormer windows, on a gable end and in the valleys and joins that are created where an extension has been added to the building. (A) shows the square hoods over the dormers; (B) illustrates the half-hipped gable end to the thatch; (C) shows both the half-hipped tip to the gable and the intricate arrangement of thatch required to make a valley between the extension to hold the large barn doors and the main building, in order to allow the rainwater to run along this and clear of the walls; (D) illustrates the large overhang required on thatch for the same purpose.*

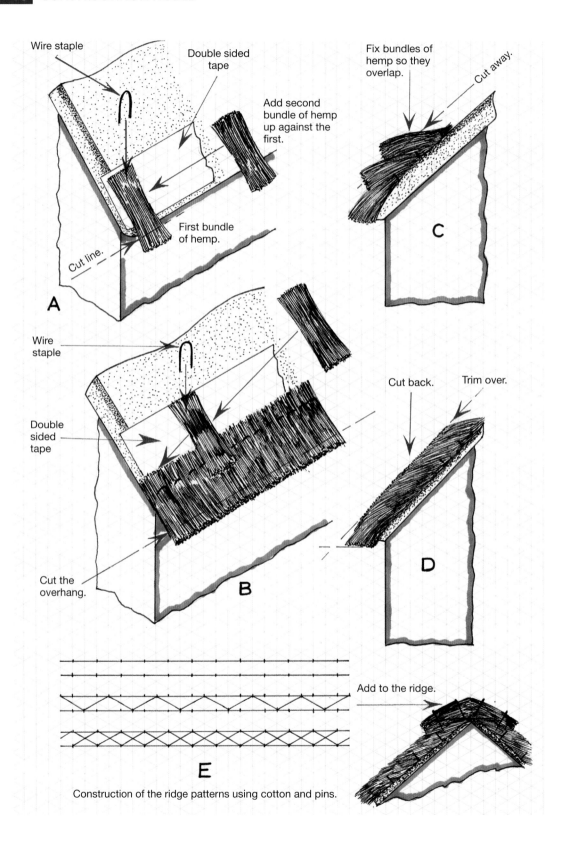

Wire staple

Double sided tape

Add second bundle of hemp up against the first.

First bundle of hemp.

Cut line.

**A**

Fix bundles of hemp so they overlap.

Cut away.

**C**

Wire staple

Double sided tape

Cut the overhang.

**B**

Cut back.

Trim over.

**D**

**E**

Construction of the ridge patterns using cotton and pins.

Add to the ridge.

strip of double-sided tape on to the sub-base. It is the same process as applying the slates and tiles. Bring each bundle to the roof and apply to the tape using tweezers. Start at the bottom edge, at the eaves, letting the first row of bundles of hemp overhang the walls. To secure, staple the bundle using a piece of small bent fine wire. This can be pushed into the exposed polystyrene foam of the sub-base. Add a little PVA to complete the fixing. Now repeat this exercise, pushing one bundle up against the next until the first row is complete. Next, move on to the second row, overlapping the first by half the length of a bundle.

Complete the second row and repeat up the pitch of the roof until you have reached the ridge. Add more PVA to secure the rows to give extra strength. The next job will be to trim the thatch back. A small pair of nail scissors is ideal for creating the trimmed finish. The ridge will require another layer of hemp, which will need to overhang and also must be carefully trimmed. Most thatched roofs are finished with an ornamental pattern of runners pegged into the thatch, which can be recreated on the model by using cotton thread. On the prototype, this would be made from hazel or willow with pegs bent from the same wood, the most common pattern being the diamond shape. Other pegs and runners are added occasionally across the bottom edge, close to the eaves. Also they are evident across the corners of hipped and half-hipped ends to the dormers. To finish the thatch, another close trim with the nail scissors will be required.

## PANTILES

Most tiles that you encounter will be of the flat or slightly curved variety. However, in some areas of the British Isles the pantile is used. This has a profile like a letter 'S' on its side. Making this type of tile for model buildings can be very difficult. It might be easier and better to use pre-cast, moulded or embossed styrene sheet, although if you are trying to recreate an old barn or cottage that has this type of tile the regimented rows of the sheets will not give the effect you are trying to replicate. In this case, you will have to try to fabricate the shape of these tiles.

The method to make this type of tile requires first making up a former. This is constructed by using the styrene pre-grooved sheet glued to a plywood or MDF base. Then fix lengths of 2.5mm-diameter styrene rod. Two of these will be needed, with the top fitting over the bottom so that the rods mesh together like a cog. Next, feed cartridge paper in-between and apply pressure to the top former using a rolling pin or something similar. This should now have created the shape to the sheet of paper. Lift the top former away, but leave the paper in position on the bottom former, brushing dilute PVA on to the paper, in order to make it more rigid. Put the paper on one side to dry off before the next stage.

The shaped paper will now require marking out into individual tiles. Remove from the bottom former and carefully cut them out. The fixing technique is more or less the same as for any other tiles, but this time they will not be required to overlap by half on the width. The rows will appear parallel with each other.

OPPOSITE: *This diagram shows how to apply the thatch to the roof. (A) After first securing it to the foam sub-base with double-sided tape, fix the first bundle at the leading edge along the line of the eaves, but overhanging the walls by about one-third of the length of the bundle. Secure it again with a piece of small bent fine wire, pushed into the foam. Lastly, secure the bundle completely to the roof with PVA glue. The next bundle can then be brought in and pushed up close to the first and secured in the same way; (B) Fix the second row in the same way as in (A) until you have completed the row. Continue on in rows until you reach the ridge; (C & D) Once the roof has been covered, it can then be trimmed; (E) This shows how to construct the runner pattern from cotton and pins; the pin heads must be cut off after completion to maintain a sense of realism. These patterns were usually to be found near to the ridge, or sometimes near to the eaves and over the corners of hipped roofs.*

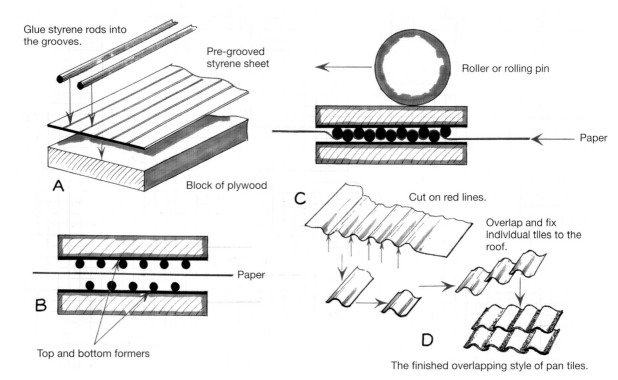

This diagram shows a method by which you can make your own pantiles. (A) First, make up a former, using pre-grooved styrene sheet and rod; (B) Here is shown how this works in profile, by offsetting the top with the bottom former so that they mesh together; a sheet of paper is then fed in-between. By exerting pressure with a rolling pin or something similar the profile shape can be achieved on the paper; (C) Take the top former away and brush some dilute PVA on to the paper in order to make it more rigid before marking and cutting out the individual tiles.

*Regimented rows of pantiles. Note that this roof must have been retiled recently as there is a definite lack of any weathering.*

## OTHER ROOF COVERINGS

Other roofing materials include corrugated metal sheet, corrugated asbestos sheet and rolled felting. The corrugated types can be fabricated in the same way as pantiles, using formers to create the shape, although this time using smaller diameter rods with closer spacing between them. For the metal sheet, try using foil instead of cartridge paper. Felting can be replicated by using masking tape, which gives a very good representation of the material; the 15mm wide tape is not far away from the width of the roll of felt in 4mm scale. The tape can be torn across the width to recreate the torn edges often seen on original buildings. This can all add to the effect you are trying to create, making your models look more authentic.

## RIDGE TILES

The next parts of the roof to consider will be the ridges, valleys and any joins. Most tiled and slated roofs will be finished at the apex with a ridge tile. There is a variety of these tiles made especially for the job and finished in blue or terracotta. The most common are the angled, or tent style; these usually come complete with a flange at one end. The other common style is the half-round. Variations of the angled tile allow for some decoration along the ridge itself. One common form is the roll top; this has a cylindrical projection at the top. More ornate forms found on estate properties have a fancy upright projection with a fretted pattern.

The common angled tile can simply be made by folding a strip of card or cartridge paper along its length. Score a line down the centre of the strip.

Hold it up to the edge of your metal ruler against the scored line and bend the material. This will ensure that the fold is straight along the length of the strip. The flanged version in 4mm scale can be produced in the same way. After it has been glued on to the ridge, small strips of card will have to be carefully glued on and spaced out at regular intervals to represent the flange. The flange creates the waterproof join from one tile to the next. The roll-top ridge tile can also be made from the strip, this time fixing a length of styrene rod into the open gap of the fold. There are some commercial etchings available from a few model suppliers representing the ornate projected ridge patterns, which can be carefully superglued into the fold's open gap.

On larger scale models, the flanged ridge tiles can be fabricated using old greetings cards again. Cut the

*(A) and (B) show the methods used to create the various ridge tiles. (A) The tent or angled style of tile; this includes the flange used on the prototype to make a watertight join; (B) The half-round type; (C) The decorative tops are added to the angled ridge tiles.*

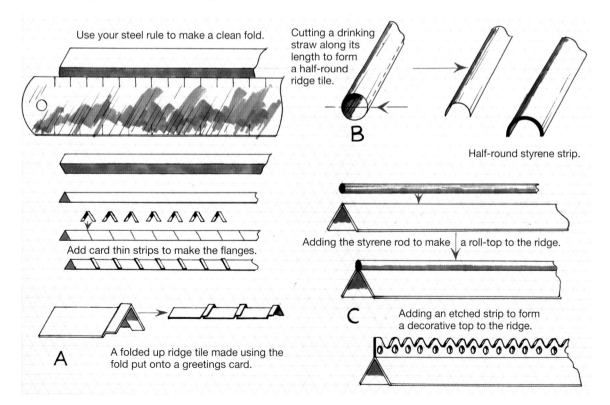

Use your steel rule to make a clean fold.

Add card thin strips to make the flanges.

A
A folded up ridge tile made using the fold put onto a greetings card.

Cutting a drinking straw along its length to form a half-round ridge tile.

B

Half-round styrene strip.

Adding the styrene rod to make a roll-top to the ridge.

C
Adding an etched strip to form a decorative top to the ridge.

*The nail shop in Belper, Derbyshire, showing the angled ridge tiles with their joining flanges.*

card right up one side of the mechanical crease put in to make the fold in the card. Mark the width of each tile, plus the length and where it will be folded. Cut all these out as individual pieces and fold up again using the metal ruler edge as an aid. Once you have cut and folded enough apply, and secure them to the ridge. If you have cut them correctly, one tile should fit over the next with the flange, just like on the prototype.

*Old Christmas cards have been used to make the ridge tiles of this Cumbrian field barn model. The lip or flange was recreated by utilizing the mechanical fold embossed into the card.* Photo: Dave Richards

*On larger-scale models, aluminium foil cut into strips makes a convincing lead flashing. Another advantage of this material is that it can be moulded around and over the slates or tiles, just like the real thing.*

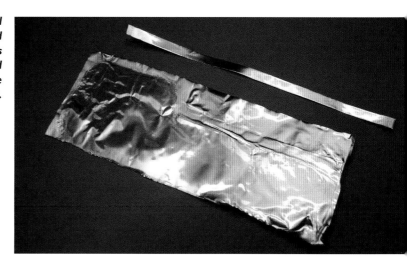

The other common ridge tile is the half-round, which can be made by carefully cutting drinking straws in half or using half-round styrene tube, the latter being the best solution for the larger scales.

## LEAD RIDGES AND FLASHINGS

Ridges, especially on hipped roofs, can be made from lead, which is usually just angled over the ridge join. However, there are some that have an ornate roll top to them. Lead is also used to form any watertight seam in the valley between two roof pitches, or on any extension or projections through the roof, such as a chimney stack.

To model flashings and ridges made from lead you can use cartridge again, or fine aluminium foil. The advantage of foil is that it can be moulded around the tiles, just like the real thing. The roll-top lead ridge strip can be produced in the same way as the roll-top tiles. On larger scales, the foil can be moulded over the top to give a very authentic finish to the model.

On older properties watertight flashings were made using cement or lime mortar. These can be replicated on your model by brushing a little of the filler plaster mix along the joint with a small amount of dilute PVA to make it runny. For unmaintained properties, add small amounts of the plaster on the

*On these cottage in Whitby, lead flashings have been used on all the joins around the dormers, the chimney stack and up to the gable parapet wall. Note also the rain staining on the pantiles; this appears as a light grey colour where it has run off the lead flashings.*

*The lead flashing and rain staining replicated on the model.*

*These are some of the many white metal chimney pots that are readily available on the market. The 7mm examples are those produced by S&D Models and the 4mm ones are from Langley Models and Shire Scenes.*

roofing material itself to represent where it has broken away and slid down the roof.

## ROOFLINES

We will now look at the details within the roof area, the most prominent feature being the chimney stacks. The stacks themselves can be modelled from the same materials used for the walls, that is, foam-board or mounting card. This will need coating with DAS for a stone stack, or the ready-mix plaster for brick or rendered finish, then scribed accordingly. The jetted brick or stonework around the top of the stack can be created from layers of mounting board cut to the relevant sizes and stacked up, then coated to match the chimney stack. Some stacks may require a plinth at the base as support, while others have a decorative string course near to the top. All of these can be made from pieces or strips of mounting card.

The top of the stack may require a chimney pot, but there are lots of stacks on rural properties that do not have them, or a simple stone or slate hood may be used instead. This can be a simple tent construction or something a little more elaborate. These can be made up from different thicknesses

*A sample prototype chimney stack with four queen pots; note also the decorative top to the ridge tiles.*

of card. The ceramic traditional pots come in many shapes and sizes, although most are either square or round in profile. You could make up chimney pots using Milliput epoxy putty, rolling the round ones and sculpting the square versions. However, there are plenty of white metal castings, including a good variety of chimney pots, on the market. The likes of S&D Models produce them in 7mm scale and for 4mm scale try Shire Scenes, Langley and Dart Castings. You should be able to find a style to match your prototype without having to fabricate one.

To secure the pots, drill a hole of an appropriate size to take the lug cast on the base of the pot. This will need to be drilled in the plinth at the top of the stack. Using superglue, fix the pot or pots into position. Once you are happy that the pot is straight, add some Milliput or DAS clay to create the flaunching. This is the build-up of cement used to secure the real pot on to the top of the stack. Milliput comes in two separate tubes, which, when mixed together, can be sculpted into shape or used as a filler. The mix will harden after a few hours, so it is important to work with it straight away.

*Two pots finish off the stack on this model of the quarry worker's cottage in Ashover, Derbyshire. This model is in 7mm scale and the pots were supplied by S&D Models.*

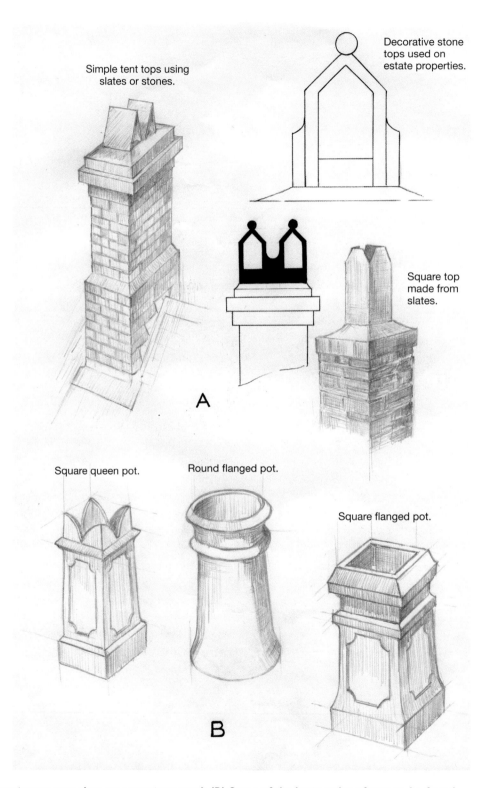

Simple tent tops using slates or stones.

Decorative stone tops used on estate properties.

Square top made from slates.

A

Square queen pot.

Round flanged pot.

Square flanged pot.

B

*(A) Alternatives to pots that are sometimes used; (B) Some of the basic styles of pots to be found.*

## BARGEBOARDS, SOFFITS, FACIAS AND FINIALS

Some rural buildings feature decorative wood-work to the roofline, although this would mainly be restricted to the estate properties where image mattered. Bargeboards provide the decorative finish to a gable end. The straight designs can be easily made from card or styrene strip; the scalloped designs can be carefully cut from card or styrene again. If you are going to require a few, it would be sensible to make a template first, then cut them out around it. Care and a reasonable amount of skill will be required to achieve a successful result. An alternative, but more expensive, method would be to draw the profile of the board. This can be drawn larger than you require, making things a little easier. Next, you can send your drawing away to have photo-etchings made. For the larger scales, a laser-cutting service could be used. Both these services will be able to reduce your drawing to its correct size, but you must indicate what that finished size should be. For the 7mm scale modeller there are a few white-metal castings available from S&D Models; like the chimney pots, you might be lucky and find a ready-made bargeboard style to suit your needs.

Some of the more decorative designs will also be finished with a finial. Making these can also prove to be rather difficult. You could try to carve one from a square-profiled length of styrene strip and then with a needle file, carefully shape it to the final finish. The alternative is to use pre-made samples cast in white metal; S&D provide them in 7mm scale.

## GUTTERING, DOWNPIPES AND RAIN HOPPERS

All rooflines apart from thatch and some barns feature guttering and downpipes to take the rainwater off the roof and away from the building. The square-profiled guttering can be made up from styrene strip; the half-round can be made from cutting drinking straws along their length, although this will only work on the larger scales (7mm and above). For 4mm and 2mm there is available a half-round beading strip produced in styrene from the Evergreen range. It is solid rather than a channel in profile, but all that is required is to paint the flat top a darker shade than the outside; at the smaller scale no one should notice. The joints or collars for square and half-round guttering can be made from thin strips of masking tape. Adding these will just give them that realistic finishing touch.

The downpipes can be made from styrene rod, obtainable from Plastrut, Evergreen and Slater's. The square type can be made from their ranges of square-profile strip. You will need to create swan necks in both profiles of pipe. For the round ones, the rod needs to be softened before bending in a small vice, using soft-grip pliers (the bent-nose style will give more control of this operation). Make two near right-angle bends to create the right shape. Add the masking-tape strip again for the joining collars. Wrap them around at least twice to give a good result, adding a little PVA to secure them. The square versions will have to be cut at a 30-degree angle to form the swan-neck bend. The square collars can be fabricated from relevant-sized styrene micro-strip.

Fitting the downpipes to the wall requires a space between the wall and the pipe itself. Small pieces of styrene strip can be used as packing pieces. On larger scales, drill a small hole into the pipe's side and likewise a matching one in the wall. Insert a fine cut-down dressmaker's pin in the hole in the pipe before supergluing into place. Carefully locate the other end of the pin into the wall and superglue this. You will need at least two pins, one near the top and one near the bottom.

The guttering will in most cases fix up to a facia board running the length of the eaves. However, a good number of our rural buildings do not have soffits and facia boards. The guttering will be suspended on brackets that are positioned away from the wall and in line with the overhang of the roof covering, which is tricky to recreate on a model. However, using a series of cut-down pins located in small holes drilled into the wall can give a realistic effect when the guttering strip is superglued to them. An alternative, but rather fiddly, method is to use small etched brass brackets superglued to the

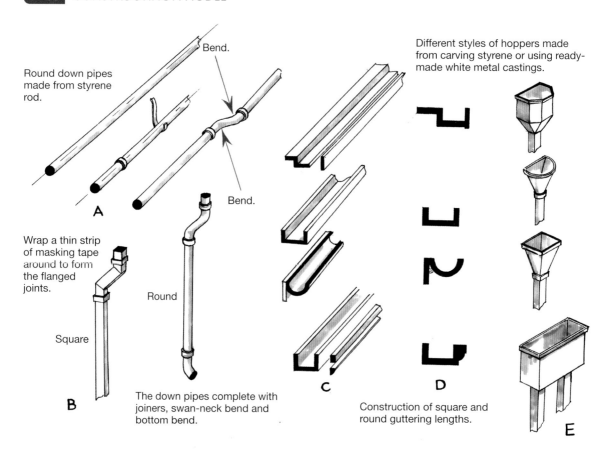

Round down pipes made from styrene rod.

Bend.

Different styles of hoppers made from carving styrene or using ready-made white metal castings.

Bend.

**A**

Wrap a thin strip of masking tape around to form the flanged joints.

Round

Square

**B**

The down pipes complete with joiners, swan-neck bend and bottom bend.

**C**

**D**

**E**

Construction of square and round guttering lengths.

*(A) shows how the swan necks can be formed as well as making up the joining collars in a round profile pipe; (B) illustrates the same but in a square-profile pipe; (C & D) show how the different profiles of guttering strip can be made up from styrene strip; (E) shows the many styles of rain hopper used. These are usually to be found where two pipes meet to cope with the extra rainwater.*

wall with the guttering suspended and attached to these. You might be able to find such brackets in the Langley range, or other etched brass suppliers.

Before concluding this section, mention must be made of rainwater hoppers. These are found at junctions or at the top of a pipe to allow the build-up of water to run away without overflowing. There are many designs for these, so look at your prototype. To model them, you could try carving them from balsa wood or styrene, or sculpting them using Milliput. In the 7mm scale, a few designs are available from S&D models in white metal. I have never seen

*Here the drainpipe arrangement can be seen with a hopper included on the gable end of this model pub.*

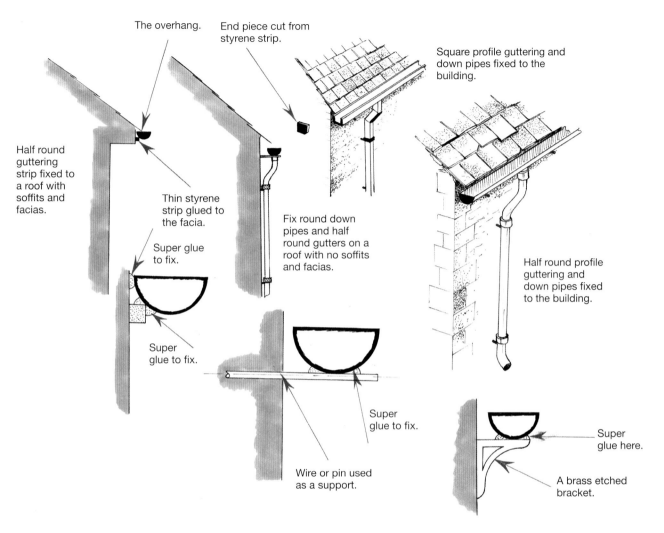

The overhang.

End piece cut from styrene strip.

Square profile guttering and down pipes fixed to the building.

Half round guttering strip fixed to a roof with soffits and facias.

Thin styrene strip glued to the facia.

Super glue to fix.

Fix round down pipes and half round gutters on a roof with no soffits and facias.

Half round profile guttering and down pipes fixed to the building.

Super glue to fix.

Super glue to fix.

Wire or pin used as a support.

Super glue here.

A brass etched bracket.

*This diagram shows the suggested ways of fixing the guttering lengths and the downpipes to the roofline. These will need to be fixed securely as they are prone to damage when handling.*

any off-the-shelf hoppers in 4mm, but there might be something out there.

This now concludes the construction of the outside of our rural buildings. All that remains is for you to paint and weather your building, which will bring it to life. We will look at this in the following chapter.

## INTERIORS

But before we move on, let's consider the interiors of our model buildings. You will have to ask yourself how far you would like to take your model and whether it's worth taking the time and effort to create a detailed interior that cannot be seen when looking through a window because it is too dark inside. There are exceptions, of course; your building might have large window apertures, allowing enough light into the interior, or at a larger scale the

*In this photograph, the net curtains are clearly visible behind the glass, so there is no reason why they should not be included on a model.*

interior will likely be visible. Finally, you might want to include lighting inside your model.

In such situations, you will have to look at modelling interiors as well. It is best to keep it simple and just model what will be seen through the windows. Start with painting the walls, then build up from mounting card the furniture that would be visible. Details on the walls such as clocks, pictures and mirrors can be modelled. Use cut-out images from magazines or brochures for the pictures and aluminium foil for the mirrors. If a chimney is situated close to a window, the chimney breast and fireplace will need to be modelled inside.

Interior details can be masked by placing curtains in your model's windows. These will also add character to the building. Simple net curtains can be made from two-ply tissue paper, separated to a single sheet. This gives a very good representation when fixed up to the inside of a window. Thicker drapes can be cut from coloured papers, such as crêpe paper available from any good arts and crafts supplier. If you are going to include curtains on your model, fit them after putting the windows into position but before placing the roof. Use either double-sided tape or a spray adhesive such as Spray Mount for this job.

If you choose to add lighting to your model, use a low-voltage bulb. Avoid lighting that is too bright, as this will only flood the model's interior and make any small gaps and imperfections obvious. Also be aware of the scale of your model and light it with an appropriate bulb. Experiment with different bulbs to see which gives the most realistic effect.

*The old and dirty nets have been reproduced on this crofter's cottage. Tissue paper proved to be a good choice to replicate them.*

# CHAPTER FOUR

# FINAL PAINTING, WEATHERING AND FINISHING

The final stage to finish your model will be the painting, weathering and adding those last little touches. This stage will require as much effort and attention to detail as any other stage, if not more. After all, the painting and finish of the model will be the first thing that will be seen. It does not matter how well the model has been built, if the painting and finish are shoddy it will not look the part. By observing the real thing and taking your time you should be able to replicate the colours and textures on your miniature versions as close as possible.

Enamels, watercolours and acrylics can all be used to paint models, but I have found that the best results overall come from using artist's oil paints. They mix well to give all those shades required, at the same time giving a textured finish when used nearly dry. I work from a range of about fifteen colours from the tube (see Appendix: Colour Reference Guide for suggestions of where and how to apply them). Most of the colours that you will use for the building materials will need to be mixed together on a

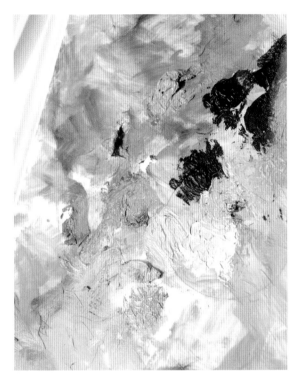

*The oil paint is then mixed on the palette to the shades required.*

*The basic colours are put out on to a plastic tub lid used for a palette.*

*A view looking into the station on the author's 7mm narrow gauge project, Ashover Butts.* Photo: Dave Richards

palette. You don't need to buy something special; the plastic lids of old ice cream tubs work well if you have these to hand. Squeeze out a little paint from each of the tubes on to the palette, then mix to the desired tones from these colours. Putting out more white is recommended as this will be used all the time to lighten the shades.

The first painting stage has been explained in Chapter 3. Now we need to look at painting the face to all the masonry.

## PAINTING EXTERIORS

### STONEWORK

In order to paint stone, start by looking carefully at your photographs, then try to mix the basic shade.

Payne's Grey, Yellow Ochre, Light Red, Raw Umber, Naples Yellow and Titanium White should give you the colour of most of the stone to be found in this country. Once you are happy with the colour, leave it out for a day until it is almost dry, then apply it over the raised surface of the stonework using a 1/8in chisel brush or a filbert brush. This dry-brush technique will put the paint on to the face of the stone, while leaving the pre-painted gaps or mortar lines untouched. You will need to go over this a few times, building up the shades within each individual block of stone; keep referring back to your reference photographs. However, do not fall into the trap of trying to pick out each individual stone in one shade only and the next one to it in a slightly darker or lighter shade, as the finished result will then resemble artificial stone cladding rather than the real thing.

The prototype of a Derbyshire gritstone wall. Note all the shades that will need to be replicated just within this small section.

Replicating the colour of the gritstone on the cottage in Ashover.

This photograph shows the prototype limestone wall of a barn in the Yorkshire Dales. Again, note the shades within the rock – it is definitely not just one colour.

Here this limestone has been replicated on this model of a field barn. Careful observation of the real thing, combined with time spent mixing and applying the colour, can give convincing results.

Another view of a barn in Dent Dale showing the rustic qualities of this rural building – perfect subject matter for a model.

Replication of the limestone, again on the barn attached to the crofter's cottage.

*Look at all the shades to this wall of old brickwork – just the same as with the stonework, careful mixing and application can result in a good replication.*

## BRICKS

We will now look at how to replicate the colour of brickwork. The techniques and mixing stage will be more or less the same as with stone. Most facing bricks will vary in shade across each individual brick – the firing of bricks created varying colours coming out from the minerals within the clay.

Red-coloured bricks can be created by using Indian Red or Light Red as the basic colour. The yellow and brown clays can be created by using Yellow Ochre, Raw Sienna, Burnt Sienna and Raw Umber. These again are only the basic colours; others will need to be added to obtain a realistic effect.

*The brick tones have been carefully picked out using shades mixed up on the pallet.*

*A good mixture of shades is seen in this barn wall. Note the differences between the new brickwork in contrast with the old.*

BELOW: *This is a good example of rendering coming away from the brick skin of the building underneath. Note the different shades within both materials.*

*This brick wall is of a lighter orange shade, although the odd darker shade appears within it.*

## RENDERING, PLASTER AND COB

The technique and colours for painting rendering, plaster and cob will be the same. Mix the colour up on the palette to the shade of the prototype. This time, you will need to add a good amount of turpentine or thinners to create a thin wash of the paint. Apply it to the walls using a 1/4in or 5mm filbert brush. Make sure you that you get the paint wash into the corners of the panels in-between the wood framing of half-timbered walls; also be careful not to get any paint on window frames or doors. This colour wash will soak into the plaster mix or DAS

*Replication of the effect of rendering coming away from the building. This was achieved using oil paint.*

clay, giving an instant effect. The paints to use are Yellow Ochre, Naples Yellow and Titanium White, although of course there are other colours and shades, like the Suffolk Pinks. You will need to go over the colours again, but this time brush the paint on dry. This will give a texture to the surface and a more authentic finish.

## TIMBER FRAMING AND CLADDING

Oak timber framing is usually finished in black or brown, but this tends to weather back to a grey shade in time. Mix the colour required using oil paint and put on with a small brush; the paint consistency needs to be a little wet when applying. Use a fine black fibre pen to line in the edges to the timbers

*A small Prairie Tank passes the signal box, heading the local stopping train towards Tawcombe Station.*

*Woodwork, like this lean-to farm shed, tends to bleach in the sunlight to a greyish-silver colour. This too can be replicated on the model by a dry-brushing technique over a base colour.*

*These lap-boarded panels have weathered to greyish-silver.*

first. This will ensure the best results, by containing the paint on the timbers and not allowing it to stray on to the panels in-between. The silvering or greying of the timbers will be covered under weathering effects later in this chapter.

Horizontal overlapped cladding can be painted in the same way as the timber framing. If other colours are required, mix them on the palette first wet then dry-brush over. This technique applies to any other timber-boarded cladding.

*This photograph shows not only the weathering to the lap boarding, but also the rusting metal clutter outside the forge. All such reference material is worth observing for possible inclusion in your models.*

*A view looking down towards the Butts coal yard.* Photo: Dave Richards

## PAINTING ROOFING MATERIALS

### SLATES AND TILES

Slate will vary in colour depending on the area from which it was quarried. For example, the slate from North Wales will be a mauve or blue shade, while that from the South West and the Lake District tends to be more green and brown in colour.

To make a start with painting slates, first put down a base colour. This can be one shade of grey; a neutral colour will create the base for all the different shades of slates found around the country. This can be applied with a brush using oil paint, or you could use one of the acrylic spray paints. Try using Halford's Matt Grey primer for lighter slate, or Humbrol Matt Tank Grey for darker shades. Both of these come in aerosol cans. If using spray paints, you must mask off all parts of the model except the roof.

Once a base colour has been applied and is dry enough, you can move on to building up the colour shades of each individual slate. Put out the basic colours from the tubes on your palette. For green slates use Terra Verte as the main colour; for the blue slates use Cobalt Blue. The mauve slates can be painted using Cobalt Violet Hue or Permanent Mauve.

Apply the paint with a flat chisel brush or a filbert brush. Use the basic colours to pick out individual slates in a random application. Once you are happy that you have created the desired random pattern, mix the basic colours with Titanium White, Naples Yellow, Yellow Ochre, Raw Umber and Payne's Grey. Use different variations of the mix to lighten, warm or darken the basic shades. Keep mixing the colours all the time and when applying them blend them into the slates until you have created a slated roof covering that is representative of the prototype. However, you will still have to weather this down to create the total finished effect.

Tiles will require painting in the same way as the slates, with a base colour being laid down first. Use Humbrol Matt Tank Grey for the Staffordshire Blue tiles and Halford's Red Oxide primer for any terracotta or red handmade tiles.

Now put out the basic oil paint colours on to your mixing palette. This time use Cobalt Violet Hue or Permanent Mauve and Prussian Blue for the Staffordshire tiles. For terracotta pantiles and hand-made tiles start with Indian Red or Warm Red for the base colours, the same as creating the colours for red brick. Apply the basic colour as before with the slates in a random pattern. Then go through the same process using the same colours to build up the final effect. Again, you will still have to add the weathering to complete the final appearance of your roof.

## THATCH

Thatch, being a natural material, will change colour with age. For a new thatched roof you will need to replicate the light straw colour. Start with Yellow Ochre, then add a little Naples Yellow and lighten with Titanium White. Thin it down with plenty of turpentine or thinners, then apply with a half-inch filbert brush, letting the colour soak into the plumber's hemp.

For more weathered and decaying thatch, use the same colours but add some Burnt Umber and Payne's Grey to darken the tone. Then add more Titanium White to bleach the thatch, giving it that aged appearance. Apply in exactly the same way using a wash of the colour. Always refer to photographs of the desired thatch you are trying to replicate.

## OTHER ROOF COVERINGS

Corrugated metal roofs will need a primer or base colour applying first. If using spray paints, they are the same as for slates and tiles above. Use grey shades for new sheets and Red Oxide if replicating old sheets that have started to rust. Mix up the colours on the palette using Payne's Grey, Titanium

*The baseboard containing the 7mm narrow gauge model of Ashover Butts. The stone-built quarry worker's cottage can be seen in its final position.* Photo: Dave Richards

*Great Western Railway Collett Goods drifts over the River Taw, on the author's 4mm scenic Dartmoor layout Tawcombe.* Photo: Steve Flint, courtesy of Railway Modeller *magazine*

White and Naples Yellow for newish sheets. For old rusted sheets, use the same colours first, but then add Light Red, Yellow Ochre and Chrome Orange. These colours can be dry-brushed on to give the best results.

Asbestos sheets both flat and corrugated can be painted first with the light grey primer, then use Payne's Grey, Titanium White and Naples Yellow, and dry-brush this on as before.

Pitched felting is painted using Humbrol Matt Tank Grey sprayed on first using the aerosol. Add to this a mix of Payne's Grey, Titanium White and a little Naples Yellow. Again use the dry-brush technique to apply this.

All the time you are mixing and applying the colours to your model use the reference photographs of the prototype and match the colours as close as possible.

## WOODWORK AND METALWORK

The window frames will have already had the colour added to them with the Promarker pens, but the doors will need to be painted. Once again, oil paint is recommended, matching the colour by mixing on the palette. Barge and soffit boards, porch support brackets and any other wood features will all also need to be painted.

Now turn your attention to painting the metalwork, such as guttering, drainpipes and any rain hoppers. It is a good idea to paint these with an undercoat or primer before adding the finishing colour. Other metalwork to pick out will be door and window furniture, together with tie-bar plates if they are fitted to your building. Match the colours for all these using your photographic references.

Chimneys conclude the basic painting. The stacks will be painted using the same techniques as for the walls. The flaunching can be picked out mixing a cement colour from Naples Yellow, Payne's Grey and Titanium White. Chimney pots can be painted by mixing and matching colours. Use Light Red and Titanium White for the terracotta versions and Yellow Ochre and Naples Yellow for the others.

## WEATHERING AND FINISHING

Once the basic painting has been completed, you can now look at adding the weathering to your building. This is the final painting stage and is the one that will really bring your model to life. All the weathering techniques described here will be executed using oil paint applied with a brush or with your fingers. I do not use an airbrush, but if you happen to possess one there is no reason not to use it. For example, it may work well in replicating the build-up of grime.

### WALLS

We will start with the walls. Mix up a little Payne's Grey with Burnt Umber and apply by using a 2mm chisel brush. Start at the top of the wall and drag the paint in a downwards direction. This will represent the staining on the walls. Use this technique again for the rain staining running off the window sills. By adding some Yellow Ochre to the mix this will replicate the algae that appear when the area is damp. Algae can usually be seen where a gutter or downpipe has leaked water down the wall.

Another form of weathering to the walls is where the lime has stained out of the lime mortar of the stone or brickwork. Use the same technique, but this time apply Titanium White, mixed with the smallest amount of Payne's Grey and Naples Yellow. Also try using your finger instead of the brush. Add the paint to the area, then drag the paint down with your finger; this can look very effective.

### WOODWORK

Various weathering effects can be seen on doors. The build-up of dirt at the bottom of a door can be replicated by dry-brushing a mix of Payne's Grey and Yellow Ochre to the area. If the door has been exposed to the damp, algae can build up. In order to create this effect, instead of using Yellow Ochre mix up some Chrome Yellow or Lemon Yellow with the grey.

Unpainted doors will bleach in the sunlight and will eventually take on a silvering effect. To achieve this, first coat the door with Payne's Grey and Yellow Ochre. When nearly dry, brush some dry

*The weathering to the door of Gorse Mill is interesting, with the green algae established on the boards.*

*The effect is recreated on the model of Gorse Mill.*

*The door from the barn in Dent Dale, showing sun bleaching. Also note the rotting of the boards at the bottom, all good material for a model.*

*The bleached effect is recreated on the model of the crofter's cottage.*

Titanium White on top. The silvering effect can also be achieved by brushing some white powder or chalk over the top of the base colour. There will also probably be a build-up of dirt around the hinges and other metalwork; rust staining can also appear around metal parts. The dirt can be mixed from the same colours as before, but this time it will need to be applied using a small brush. For the rust staining, use a little Light Red and Chrome Orange and again use the small brush.

The effect of paint the blistering on doors can be achieved by using masking tape. Paint the door first in the undercoat or natural wood colour. Then paint on the top colour of the door and just before the

*The build-up of dirt has been reproduced lightly on this cottage door.*

*A close-up of the door of the barn in Dent Dale, illustrating the blistering of the paint on the doors.*

paint has completely dried off put a piece of masking tape on to the surface of the painted door. Now quickly rip the masking tape away. This should take some of the paint away and leave the rest on the door, creating the blistered paint effect.

Weathering timber frames on buildings can be done in the same way as on the boarded doors. To achieve the effect of the wood being bleached, use chalk powder or the residue from scribing out the clay. On smaller-scale half-timbered buildings try using a white or light grey pencil crayon. Rub this on to the dark colour of the pre-painted timbers to create the bleached effect.

## THE ROOF

The tile and slate covering to a roof will weather more or less in the same way. The roof materials will soon show signs of weathering from rain staining. This will appear in streaks running down from the ridge to the eaves. To replicate this, use the Payne's Grey mixed with a little Burnt Umber, then apply this either using a brush or by dragging the paint down the roof with your finger. The same technique can be used for the staining that comes off the lead flashing. This time though use Titanium White with a little Naples Yellow added.

The other obvious weathering to be seen on roofs is a build-up of lichens and mosses. These can usually be found growing on the edge and ridge. They start to grow from where birds have landed and the droppings they produce, which act as a fertilizer for this algae growth to multiply.

The common types you will see on the roof are usually orange, ochre or pale green in colour. To create the orange variety, use Chrome Orange; for ochre use Yellow Ochre; and for the pale green use Sap Green with a little Titanium White added to lighten it. Apply this to your building's roof using an old brush with the bristles cut back to about 5mm from the ferrule. Load the brush with paint, then apply it to your model using a stipple action.

Lichens are not always confined to the roof; they can also be seen growing on walls, especially on stone ones. The stipple action can be used as above, or wetter paint can be applied by loading an old toothbrush with the colour and flicking it from the brush on to the model.

Corrugated roofing materials will weather in the same way. Corrugated asbestos supports the growth of lichens and mosses. However, corrugated metal sheeting will deteriorate in our climate. It will not be long before it will oxidize and a coating of

*A BR Standard class 5 MT runs through the station on Julian Birley's magnificent 7mm model Evercreech New. The author was responsible for hand-painting the back scene.* Photo: Andy Colson

*The rain staining is again obvious on this barn roof. Note the blistered paint on the removed door in the foreground.*

*This is a very good example of the effects of rain staining on a roof. Note also the build-up of the brightly coloured lichens growing on the ridge and the sides of this farm outbuilding in Beeley, Derbyshire.*

**Rust can be seen on the old corrugated sheeted roof of the cart shed on this model of Belstone Farm.**

rust will take over. This effect can be replicated using paint. Start with the Red Oxide spray undercoat. Mix Chrome Orange with Yellow Ochre and brush this all over. Try using the stipple brush technique, as this can give the effect of the rust layering and breaking away from the surface.

Thatch will also weather, but with mosses and fungi rather than lichens taking hold. To create this effect on the model, finely grated foam flock is recommended for the mosses. Fungi can be stippled on using Titanium White, Naples Yellow and Yellow Ochre, either straight from the tubes or mixed together. Always look at the real thing and try to match what you see. This brings us nicely to the final stage of weathering, with plant life making an appearance on the model buildings.

## VEGETATION AND PLANT LIFE

The plant life seen on our rural buildings comes into two categories. First are the plants that have been purposely grown to decorate and break up the lines of the property. If this is the case, the owner will

**S&D 7F in charge of a train of coal empties trundles though Evercreech New station on Julian Birley's model.**
Photo: Andy Colson

*Rain staining and lichen are reproduced on the model of the crofter's cottage and barn.*

keep this growth in check, sometimes manicuring it to an extreme. Others might let the plants grow wilder over their property. The idyllic image of a thatched cottage with rambling roses around the door is what most of us associate with the English countryside.

The second category is where the growth of plant life is not in any way kept in check. The plants have been left to take over. This type of vegetation will only be seen on the less well-maintained buildings and those that have been abandoned and are derelict. Buildings that have been shrouded in this type

*This photograph shows the coming together of two roofing materials used on the roofs of the high and low barns on the model of the farm. Note the blending of colour used on the tiles and again on the thatch. Both have been weathered down to give an aged look.*

*Another view of the two barns, showing the painting effects in more detail.*

of wild vegetation can take on a dark and mysterious ambiance.

Both types of plant life can be replicated on our models using scenic materials. I use the range provided by Woodland Scenics, although I have also from time to time used those manufactured by NOCH, Heki, Green Scene or Treemendus.

Convincing ivies and other creepers can be created by taking the foam flock that comes on matting and teasing it apart a little. It can then be fixed to the

*In this view of a model barn, the build-up of lichens is evident on the roof and down to the eaves. This was achieved by stippling the paint nearly dry on to the model.*

ABOVE: *A Standard 2-6-2 tank heads a local away from Evercreech New.* Photo: Andy Colson

BELOW: *The plant growth on this cottage has clearly been manicured by the owner to give a neat finish.*

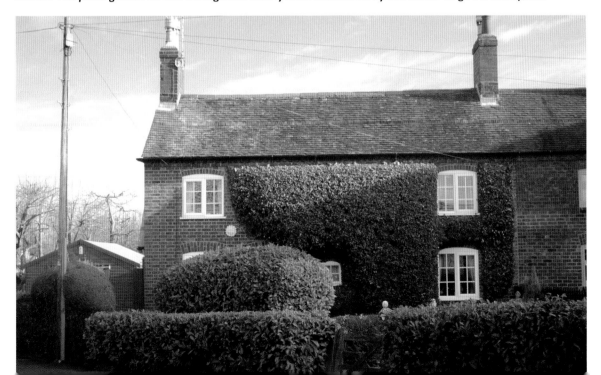

The ivy on this barn has been left to run wild.

Ivy is seen creeping its way up the walls and over the roof of this farm outbuilding. This always looks good when recreated on a model.

The ivy growing on this dilapidated wooden cart shed is probably holding it together! The building has an interesting lean to it, which is worth considering incorporating on a model.

*On this 7mm model the ivy growing up the side of the barn has been created by using the bracts from silver birch catkins, as they look very convincing in this scale. They were attached to the walls and roof using PVA glue, before being sprayed with a matt varnish to prevent them from rotting away.*

building using a spray adhesive such as Spray Mount. On larger scale models from 7mm upwards, ivy can be formed by using the natural bracts found in the catkins of the silver birch tree – these bracts are identical to the large ivy leaf. You can collect them yourself and dye them, or they can be purchased ready-coloured from Green Scene. To fix to the building, use a spray adhesive or PVA.

There may be other plant life on your buildings, such as grasses that have seeded themselves. Study the prototype to see where such growth appears. Guttering is a common place to see grass as it seeds itself into the silt that tends to build up, especially at the end of a gutter section.

Different materials can be used to create a variety of grasses. Carpet underlay felt can be used by teasing

*Here on the 4mm model of the farm's thatched barn, ivy has been created from one of the foliage mats produced by Woodland Scenics. This material looks very convincing at this scale.*

This model of a derelict field barn on Bonsall Moor, Derbyshire. In this dilapidated state, Mother Nature has really started to take over, with ivy, weeds, grass and even a small hawthorn bush taking root. These have all been recreated by using different scenic materials, including carpet underlay felt, teddy bear fur, horse hair, grated foam flock and finally static nylon grass fibres.

The prototype of the larger of the two derelict barns – there is plenty of evidence of nature taking over on this building.

it back to its raw fibres – when painted this can look very effective. For longer grass, try teddy bear fur or the modelling product static grass, although you will need to buy the applicator for this. All these can be glued using a PVA adhesive. (All of the materials above were used to dress the model of the derelict Derbyshire field barn.)

Brightly coloured fine foam can be used to create flowers, which are then added to the green matt flock using a spray adhesive or hairspray. Fine pink or white foam flock can be used to represent the proverbial roses growing around a cottage door. Another way of producing smaller flowers on creepers is to use fine dyed sawdust; this works well to represent bindweeds.

This now brings your model building to completion. It has been painted, weathered and dressed with foliage. All you have to do now is to set the building into the scenery.

*An idyllic village scene with thatched cottages nestling together. All the cottages have some sort of growth growing on or around them, making them blend in with their surroundings.*

# CHAPTER FIVE

# SETTING YOUR MODEL BUILDING INTO THE LANDSCAPE

It has long been accepted that the vernacular architecture of our rural buildings is in perfect harmony with the landscape. Indeed, some of the most famous masterpieces of art feature buildings set into the landscape. *The Hay Wain* by John Constable is a good example of this. A century later artist Helen Allingham captured the romantic thatched cottages with roses around the door that nestled within the British landscape, inspiring many a chocolate-box image. Another example of rural buildings appearing as commercial pieces of art were those to be found under the luggage racks decorating railway carriages in the past.

As modellers we are trying to create the same visual images, although we are creating them in three dimensions rather than two, and our blank canvas is the baseboard. The best model railways are those that have considered the landscape – after all, the landscape was there first with the railway built into it, not the other way around. The best example of this is 'The Vale Scene' at Pendon Museum in Oxfordshire. This is a wonderful depiction of the English countryside during the early 1930s, faithfully captured in miniature with its cottages and farms and a railway running through it. A visit is strongly recommended for any modeller.

Rural buildings that have been abandoned and are derelict blend perfectly into the landscape. Artists have long used these ruins to depict romantic and picturesque scenes. For us modellers, derelict buildings always provide very interesting subject matter for a model railway, fitting in with all periods.

All of the buildings described in this book have a little extra added to the depth of the walls, in order to give the buildings some footings and allow them to sit into the ground around them (just like the real thing). When you come to plant your building, build the landscape up to it. You can make up a box out of card to the size and footprint of the building, or cut the footprint out of the baseboard material. Either way, the model, with its extra footings, will then slide into it with a snug fit. The join can then be filled in with a little plaster mixed with PVA, or left free. Leaving it free would be the best solution for a portable or exhibition layout, as the buildings could then be transported separately to the baseboards, avoiding damage and storage issues. It also means

*Ivy created using the foliage mat modelling product; here it has been positioned between the stable and the cart shed on the model farm. It can be used to mask an awkward join perfectly.*

*Southern Railway class T9 pulls away from Tawcombe with a local train for Bude on the North Cornish coast.*

that your building can be removed to carry out any maintenance work that it might require during its life.

## DRESSING THE MODEL

If carried out in the right way, dressing can add another dimension to your models, bringing them to life. But beware of overdoing it. I have seen countless layouts where scenes have been created but have gone over the top, making them too busy. This can make the viewer confused, taking the visual attention away from the actual buildings. The way to go about this is to create small, interesting cameo scenes, which will allow the viewer to be drawn into the rest of the three-dimensional picture that you are creating.

Everyday situations work better than dramatic scenes. If you do want to include a dramatic scene, keep it to one only. I have seen chaos created with

houses on fire at one end of the layout and a car crash at the other. Two people having a conversation over the garden gate or while walking the dog appears more natural and works much better.

There are plenty of figures manufactured in all the major scales. Dart Castings and Monty's Model Railways produce exquisite figures with all the fine detail and features reproduced for most of the 4mm/1:76 scale. There are also figures supplied by Langley Models and Springside. All these models come as unpainted, white metal castings. The larger scales are also catered for, with some superb castings, such as those produced by S&D Models for the 7mm/1:42 scale model dioramas and layouts. These figures again will require painting; a coat of primer followed by oil paints is recommended.

Other dressings might be needed to make up convincing cameo scenes. Animals can be included. Dart Castings, Shire Scenes, Langley and Springside models all produce unpainted white metal castings in

ABOVE: *These derelict barns harmonize with the landscape of the moor.*

BELOW: *This wide view, showing all of Belstone Farm, reveals how the buildings are closely grouped together and fit into the landscape around them.* Photo: Andy York, British Railway Modelling *magazine*

ABOVE: *This ruined farmhouse, isolated on Haworth Moor, West Yorkshire, takes on a mysterious ambiance.*

BELOW: *This photograph illustrates the composition of a scene. As modellers, we must try to position our models in balance with their surroundings, just as an artist would do when composing a painting. The ruined barn balances nicely with the drystone wall and drover's track in-between. The tree is positioned to complete the composition, giving height and creating scale.*

*This and the next photograph illustrate the reason for adding the extra depth to the walls of all the model buildings. You can clearly see how the footings on the building will allow it to fit into the foundation created in the scenery.*

the smaller scales. For the 7mm scale S&D Models and Duncan Models supply some excellent examples, especially farm animals including a variety of shire horses.

Besides the humans and animals, other accessories will be needed to finish the scene. For example,

if your model includes farm buildings, you will also require plenty of farm dressings. Tractors, carts and other farm machinery, as well as smaller items such as milk churns, all help to create the scene. These again are available from Dart Castings, Shire Scenes, Langley and Springside Models. For the 7mm modeller, S&D and Duncan Models both specialize in this area, with kits to make up some wonderful models.

Other items to consider are motor vehicles, push bikes, prams and wheelbarrows, or any other item with wheels, as well as accessories such as garden gates and chicken coops, not forgetting the chickens to go in them. To add details to the actual buildings, try using a tie-bar plate. This can look very convincing on an old cottage or farm building. The round type has been used on the model of the crofter's cottage and the barn, while the X-shaped one has been added to the Ashover quarry worker's cottage.

Look for photographs for reference if you are modelling the 1900s to the 1950s. You can also try looking through books containing any of the Francis Frith photographs, such as *English Villages – Classic Photographs from the Francis Frith Collection*, by Black Horse Books. You might find these photographs or others on the internet, as well as printed in books.

Setting your models into the landscape can include creating the paths and yards around the buildings. The methods and materials used here are the same as for a building's walls, but flat rather than vertical. A skin of DAS modelling clay or plaster in some cases can be used. When dry, the patterns of slabs, flags or cobbles can all be scribed out before painting and weathering them. All these extra dressings will help to set your model rural buildings off, creating the total desired scene in miniature.

*The other advantages to using this method are that it will allow you to remove the building from its foundation. This can be very useful for a portable layout, where the buildings can be transported separately from the baseboards, avoiding the risk of them getting damaged. Also, it allows for easy maintenance to take place, which the building may require from time to time.*

ABOVE: *Lacock in Wiltshire is now completely owned by the National Trust and is kept in its original condition. The village is full of buildings that would make wonderful models. Indeed, the village has been seen as the backdrop to many TV dramas and feature films in recent times.*

BELOW: *An illustration of mine of Osmaston village in south Derbyshire. Note the composition – the cottages sit nicely around the village duck pond on the green. Also note the little scene created, with the postman engrossed in conversation with the housewife over the garden gate, while he leans on his bike. The cat gives a nice touch, always in need of some fuss. These little cameo scenes can finish a model off as well as becoming a focal point.*

# CHAPTER SIX

# PROJECTS – SCRATCH-BUILDING THREE RURAL BUILDINGS

In this chapter, we will look at making three rural buildings from scratch. The first building is a country farmhouse, the selected prototype for which is a half-timbered example at Marchington in the Dove Valley, East Staffordshire. The second is a cob-built thatched cottage. This cottage is imagined, although based on actual cottages found in Devon. The last building selected is a farm building, a stone-built barn in a state of ruin. This rustic structure is one of the many limestone field barns to be found on Bonsall Moor, near Matlock in the Derbyshire Peak District.

For further details of how to construct individual parts of the models, *see* Chapter 3.

## THE COUNTRY FARMHOUSE

### REFERENCE AND PRODUCING A WORKING DRAWING

Starting with a visit to the farmhouse at Marchington, a series of photographs was taken. It was not possible to gain access to the property to take any measurements on site. The alternative therefore was to use the photographs to estimate all the measurements. Using the methods described in Chapter 2, the door was taken as a base for all the other measurements, in order to produce a drawing of 4mm to the foot scale. The drawings of the front and end elevations are included here. You will notice that the entire half-timbered box frame has been included – the reason for this will become apparent later.

*This is the prototype chosen for our first model project. The half-timbered farmhouse is situated in Marchington, east Staffordshire.*

*The working drawing was produced from all the photographs taken on site.*

## BUILDING THE SHELL

In order to achieve the close window reveals on this building, the decision was made to create the shell from two layers. The first layer was cut from 3mm foamboard. You will notice that the window apertures have been cut larger, so as to allow the windows to drop on to the pre-cut spaces; all will become clearer a little later on. The components have now been cut out with the extra centimetre to the depth of all the wall sections. This will give the building its footings.

With the foamboard components now prepared, mark and cut out the same elevations using 1.5mm mounting card, but leaving the windows and doors for the time being. The side walls have 4.5mm extra added at each end to form the wrap-around corner.

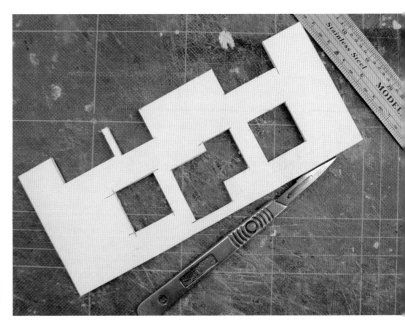

*Transfer the drawing to the 3mm foamboard and cut it out, leaving about 5mm extra around the window apertures.*

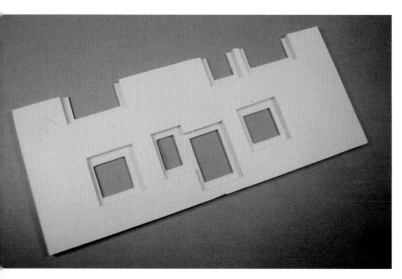

Cut out a second layer, this time from mounting card, with the window apertures cut to the actual size. Glue this to the foamboard layer.

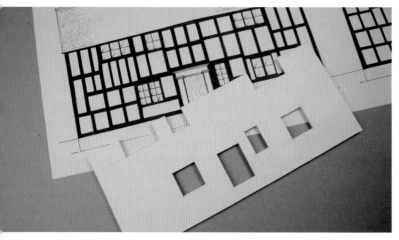

Make a same-size photocopy of all the elevations on the drawing.

Fix the photocopy to the outside card layer using spray adhesive.

*Cut out the window apertures from the photocopy on top.*

The next stage has now been reached, in which the extra detail on the drawing will be needed. Make a same-size photocopy of the elevations, cut them out and place them in position to the mounting card using spray adhesive or double-sided tape. You can now cut all the windows out using a sharp blade to the inside edge of the frames.

## CONSTRUCTING THE TIMBER FRAME

The mounting card components can now be offered up to the foamboard inner carcass and glued into position. The next stage will be to construct the timber frame. This is the reason for going to the trouble of producing it on the drawing. With the photocopies of the drawing now fixed to the building material, it will be easy to cut and assemble the timber frame directly on to it. Thin strips of balsa wood are a good material to replicate the frame. A mixture of 2mm, 3mm and 4mm strips of only 0.75mm thick will serve for all the timbering. Carefully cut these to size and glue them into position. The corner timbers will need to overlap with a butt joint.

*Assemble the timber frame directly on to the photocopy – this was the reason for taking the trouble to draw it in full.*

*Photo: Dave Richards*

*The construction of the timber frame nears completion on the front elevation. The infill to the panels has also been applied using both the DAS clay and the filler plaster.*

*A close-up showing the DAS and filler plaster making up the infill to the panels.*
Photo: Dave Richards

*The prototype of the timber frame and plaster and lath panels between. This is what we are trying to replicate on the model.*

## CREATING THE PLASTER PANELS

Once you are happy with the result, you can move on to coating the panels in-between the frames to represent the lime plaster, using plaster filler and DAS modelling clay. First, brush on the ready-mixed plaster, making sure you get into the corners; a smaller brush will give more control. When dry, add a small amount of DAS to the panels using a dentist's probe (the ones used to apply filling paste into place). Use this tool to push the clay into the corners. When all the clay is dry, do a little scribing to replicate any cracking appearing in the plasterwork.

## CONSTRUCTING THE WINDOW FRAMES

The next thing is to construct the window frames. Use old greetings cards, with double-sided tape on the reverse side to affix to the clear glazing film. The reason for cutting the window apertures oversized on the inside foamboard shell will now become apparent. The clear glazing film has been cut out about 5mm larger than the frames themselves. Put thin strips of double-sided tape on the edge of the glazing, then fix them from the back to the rear side of the mounting card, cut out to the actual size of the aperture.

*The window frames are constructed from strips of old greetings card, then assembled direct on to the glazing material, while fixed in the final position.* Photo: Dave Richards

*All the windows are now complete, so the net curtains can be added using strips of tissue paper. The door and ornate frame have also been constructed.*

*It is easier to paint the timber frame and the plaster panels before adding the windows. The windows do not need to be painted as they are white on the prototype.*

Turning over the wall components, start to assemble the window frames, using strips of card to construct the casement frames. To do this, first fix a length of double-sided tape to the back of the card as usual. Now cut the strips ready for the frames, stiles and cross-pieces. You will need to be very careful, using a series of cuts with a sharp blade. In 4mm scale, they should be no more than 1.5mm wide. Cut the stiles (or the uprights) first and fix them to the glazing, butting them up to the shallow reveals. Then cut and fix up the cross-pieces. Last of all, the glazing bars will need to be fitted into place. These are made from adhesive-backed paper labels (*see* Chapter 3).

Construct the windows using this method for all the flat components. Putting a metal rule up against the inside of the glazing will add a support for you when constructing the frames. Net curtains have been added to the windows using strips of tissue paper. If you decide to include these, fix them into position with spray adhesive or double-sided tape.

## FIXING THE DOORS

The next stage is to fix the doors into place. All the doors are vertical-boarded and are constructed in the way described in Chapter 3. The strap hinges, however, will not be required as they are fitted to the inside cross-battens and will not be visible.

With all the windows and doors fitted into position you can start to assemble all the components, gluing at the butt joints using PVA and pinning the joint until it has bonded. Use scraps of the foamboard or mounting card to provide the corner and stretcher braces.

## PAINTING THE PANELS AND TIMBER FRAME

Before fitting the roof, it is advisable to paint the panels, then the balsa wood half-timbered framework. The window frames will not require any colouring as they are painted white on the prototype, so can be left in the finish of the card. Paint the panels using Titanium White oil paint with a little Naples Yellow added to it. Moving on to the timber frame, this can either be painted using Payne's Grey and Burnt Umber mixed together, or you can use a dark wood stain. Whatever you choose, you will need to apply it using a fine one-stroke brush – no. 1 or no. 2 is recommended.

## CONSTRUCTING THE ROOF

The sub-base for the roof can now be fitted, although some strips of foamboard need to be fitted first to support it. You will notice from the photographs that the roof is not straight along the ridge. To achieve this effect, the sub-base needs to be cut to the shallow angles where they will meet at the ridge. The sub-base will therefore need to be made up from four sections to replicate the actual shape of the roof. Cut the panels from card, remembering to cut out a section for the chimney. Glue the four pieces to the gable end supports and to the top of the walls. Fix the section together using masking tape, which can also be used over the ridge.

## FITTING AND TILING THE ROOF

With the sub-base fixed and secured, the next stage is the fitting of all the roofing tiles. These will first need to be cut as individual tiles to replicate the uneven appearance of the prototype (for the cutting technique, see Chapter 3). Fix strips of double-sided tape to the sub-base and, starting at the eaves, tile the roof up to the ridge. Use a strip of card to create the visible bump and sag along the roof. Bend a thin piece of card over the strip, then tile over the top to give the finished effect.

To finish the roof all that is needed is the ridge tiles. These can be made from card by folding in tent fashion. Glue the tiles in position about 6 mm apart along the ridge with an extra thin strip of card to represent the flange.

*The construction of the building is seen in this photograph. Note the extra strips added to the gable ends to support the roof panels.*

*A sub-base is assembled from foamboard to support the roof panels and the chimney stack. One of the gable trusses is made higher than the other, because the roof pitch is higher at one end on the prototype.*

*The four roof panels are now fixed into position. All the joins have been covered with masking tape.*

## CONSTRUCTING THE CHIMNEY STACK

The main feature along the ridge of the farmhouse is the centre-positioned chimney stack. This was constructed using mount card, before covering the face with embossed brick styrene sheet. You must be careful when using this material to make sure that the coursing lines up around the corners. Alternatively, the brickwork could be scribed into a coating of plaster or thin layer of modelling clay.

## FITTING THE GUTTERING AND DOWNPIPES

The last thing to construct is the guttering and down-pipes; styrene strip and round rod have been used here. They are supported on pins fixed and secured with superglue and positioned just under the eaves. The swan necks were formed in the way described in Chapter 3.

## FINAL PAINTING AND WEATHERING

The next stage is to paint the tiled roof and chimney. Here, the whole roof is given a base coat using the Tank Grey spray paint; however, you will first have to mask off the walls that have already been painted.

Next, paint individual tiles in shades of grey, blue and mauve in a random pattern to replicate the Staffordshire tiles used on this farmhouse. Apply a light coating of dark and light grey to blend the colours together and give a more authentic and weathered look.

Turning to the chimney, apply a wash of Naples Yellow mixed with Titanium White to fill in the mortar lines. When this has dried, dry-brush over it a mix of Chrome Orange and Warm Red lightened with Titanium White. Pick out a few bricks in dark brown and white. Glue the pots into position and add a flaunching around them using a small amount of DAS clay. The pots are painted in a buff colour and the flaunching pale grey. Apply a light coat of Payne's Grey to represent the weathering and build-up of sooty grime seen at the top of the chimney stack.

Before you put your paints away, the front and other doors will need to be painted. The front door appears to be very weathered down; a mixture of Payne's Grey, Yellow Ochre and Titanium White should provide this appearance; brush on when nearly dry. Lastly, brush white talcum powder over the door and frames to give that authentic aged appearance.

## ADDING THE VEGETATION

All that remains to finish the farmhouse is to add the ivy growth to the right-hand corner of the building. A close examination of the photographs reveals just where and how extensive this growth is. In 4mm scale, flock is the best material to give the most realistic impression. Tease this away from the matting and carefully attach it to the building's walls and roof with a little spray adhesive.

## SETTING THE MODEL INTO THE SCENERY

The model of the farmhouse will look all the more realistic if set into its surroundings. The first task here is to mark the footprint of the building on to the baseboard, in this case 10mm fibre board. Cut this to shape to form the farmhouse's foundation. The photographs revealed a Yorkstone path leading to the front door. This is created using a little DAS clay and applying it very thinly into some PVA in the area required. When dry, scribe out the pattern of the stone slabs and paint them to finish. The front and rear garden area is first painted in a dark grey to represent the soil, before planting it out with shrubs and plants using different shades of green flock from the Woodland Scenics range. This now completes the first project of the model country farmhouse.

*The finished model of the farmhouse complete with the roof and chimney fully painted and weathered. Also the ivy has been added growing up the walls and on to the roof. The model has also been set into its surroundings with a stone flagged path leading up to the front door.*

## DEVON (COB) THATCHED COTTAGE

### REFERENCE AND PRODUCING A WORKING DRAWING

In this project, rather than working from an actual prototype, we will be building a model of an imagined cob thatched cottage, based on the cottages found in Devon and other counties of the West Country. The plan for the cottage has been devised from personal photographs taken while visiting Devon and by consulting books showing this type of cottage.

*A prototype of a Devon cob thatched cottage. This one at Lustleigh was used to base the model on.*

*This is the working drawing for the second project. The cottage was imaginary, but based on prototypes of similar cottages found in the West Country.*

## CREATING THE BUILDING'S SHELL

Using the working drawing, I was able to redraw the components to make up the building's main shell; 3mm foamboard was used for this. The cottage has two extensions at either end. One of these has been made of mounting card instead of foamboard, owing to its small size. There is an angled buttress wall up to the front wall, which can also be constructed from mount card. With all the components assembled together and with the window aperture and doors cut out, the next stage is to apply the skin to the building.

*One of the gable ends after it has been cut out; remember to save all the cut-away triangles for corner bracing later on.*

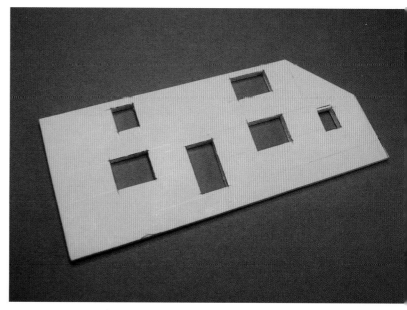

*The side elevation is cut out from 3mm foamboard.*

This photograph shows all the components laid out on the cutting board ready for assembly.

All the sides are now assembled, with the bracing added and a buttress to the left side of the front wall.

Pictured is another view of the completed carcass, ready to take the model on to the next stage.

## APPLYING THE SKIN TO THE BUILDING

The building material is cob, which is made from straw and mud. A convincing way to replicate this material is to use a combination of DAS modelling clay and No More Cracks ready-mixed plaster. The model is now given its skin. First, brush on a mix of PVA and the filler plaster. Allow this to dry, then add a thin coating of PVA glue. While this is still tacky, apply DAS modelling clay to parts of the wall in order to replicate the cob finish. With a lollipop stick, spread the clay filling in the corners. Put the whole model to one side to dry off completely.

*The model is now given its skin: first, a mix of PVA and the filler plaster was brushed on.* Photo: Dave Richards

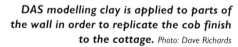

*DAS modelling clay is applied to parts of the wall in order to replicate the cob finish to the cottage.* Photo: Dave Richards

*Before adding the clay a coating of PVA will be required.* Photo: Dave Richards

## APPLYING THE BASE COLOUR

The finished skin on this model has been given a coat of base paint, with a wash made up using Titanium White with a very small amount of Naples Yellow. This colour wash represents the cob very well, without too much extra paint needed to create the finished effect.

## MAKING AND FIXING THE DOORS AND WINDOWS

Once the model is dry, the windows and doors can be added. Start with the windows, fixing the clear celluloid packaging with tape to all the apertures. Then make up the casement frames from card, as described in Chapter 3. All the doors to the cottage are of the vertical-planked variety; the latches also need to be fabricated, but the strap hinges are fixed to the inside of the door, so are not visible on the model.

## CONSTRUCTING THE SUB-BASE TO THE ROOF

A deep thatched roof is needed for this model. Start with 6mm thick foamboard; this will give the depth of thatch required. To give the thatch some shape, strip the top sheet of card away from the board, leaving the polystyrene core exposed. Cut the roof

panels to size, leaving about 12mm overlap to the eaves and at the ridge. Then cut a chamfer to both the ridge and at the eaves. The cut at the ridge is to allow both sections to come together; the cut at the eaves should be at an angle so that it remains at a right angle to the wall.

You will also notice that the roof is gabled at one end and half-hipped at the other. The half-hipped section will need to be cut from the same foamboard, then mitre-cut to join the main roof panels. Examples of half-hipped roofs and the overhang of thatch can be seen in Chapter 3.

Fix the roof panels into position using PVA glue. Use pins to secure the panels in place while the bond is forming; the pins can be fully pushed in and left in position as they will be covered by the thatching. Add more PVA along the ridge to make the join more secure, then leave everything to properly dry off.

Picking up the model after a few hours have passed, you can move on to the shaping. To give some shape to the sub-base for the thatch, first carve it with a very sharp blade in the scalpel. Follow this by sanding both edges and the ridge to round them off. The panels can also be given a light sanding down. This will prepare the roof panels for the thatch to go on top.

*The sub-base of the thatch roof is being cut from 6mm foamboard. The sides of the panel require cutting at an angle so that they will come together at the ridge.*

Photo: Dave Richards

Here the top sheet of card can be seen being pulled away from the board to reveal the foam core underneath.

*Photo: Dave Richards*

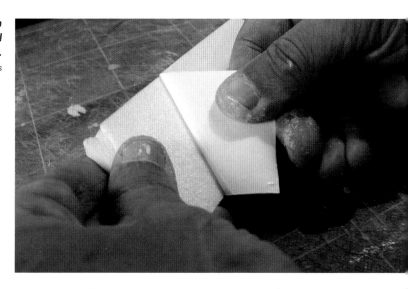

The foamboard roof panels are now fixed into position using PVA glue. The joins will need to be pinned until the glue has bonded.

*Photo: Dave Richards*

The roof panels in position with the pins securing them. They can be left in position as the thatch will cover them.

*Photo: Dave Richards*

*The edges are trimmed and carved to shape. This will give a good base for application of the thatch.*
Photo: Dave Richards

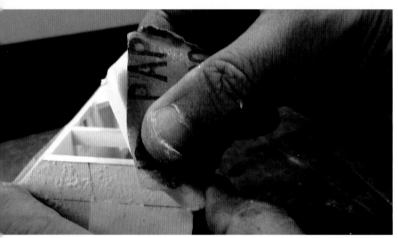

*The edges and the ridge of the roof panels are sanded down and shaped before the thatch is added.*
Photo: Dave Richards

*The finished roof panels now await the addition of the thatch.*
Photo: Dave Richards

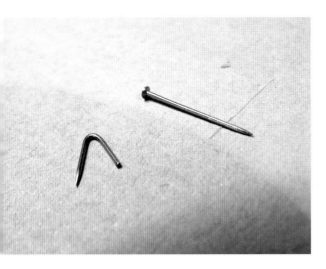

***Making staples from small pins.*** *Photo: Dave Richards*

## APPLYING THE THATCH TO THE ROOF

The thatch for this cottage is made from plumber's hemp. The first task is to cut small bundles of the hemp from the scathe. These should be no longer than 15mm; cut about a dozen at a time to work with. The next job is to cut and bend some fine fuse wire or a pin to make some staples. You will need a good number of these to fix the thatch bundles to the roof panels.

Pick the first bundle up using a pair of tweezers and position this in the corner, along the level of the eaves, but overlap the edge by about 5mm. Then insert a staple to fix the bundle to the roof; this will push into the polystyrene foam with ease. It is a good idea to add some PVA glue to make the fixing secure. Repeat this exercise along the bottom row, but make sure that each bundle butts up to the previous one.

Once the bottom row is complete, fix the second row. This will need to overlap the first by about 5mm. Starting at the same corner go along the row, fixing the bundles in the same way. Repeat this until you have reached the ridge. It may be necessary to brush some dilute PVA over the rows of hemp to bond together. Leave this for a while for the PVA to set solid.

The next stage is to trim off the surplus hemp at the eaves and tidy up any other areas, including the ridge, before putting the extra layer of hemp over the ridge itself. This will need trimming once it has been successfully secured.

To finish off the construction of the thatch, the runner pattern can be added. Cotton thread is ideal for this. First pin it into position, then secure it to the thatch with dilute PVA glue. You will have to be patient, but if you do take your time a successful result can be achieved.

***The first bundle of thatch is offered up into position and secured with double-sided tape and a staple.*** *Photo: Dave Richards*

**The hemp bundle is secured finally with PVA glue.**

Photo: Dave Richards

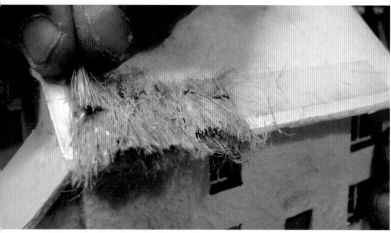

**The second row of hemp is added, first being secured with a staple and then with PVA glue. Apply this technique until the hemp has reached the ridge.**

Photo: Dave Richards

**The thatch can be trimmed to shape using nail scissors.**

Photo: Dave Richards

*The finished thatch on the model, created using the plumber's hemp and now all trimmed at the edges.*

*This close-up shows the thatch at the final stage, that of adding the hazel runners. They are created here on from cotton and glued into position with PVA.*

## CONSTRUCTING THE CHIMNEY STACKS

The last items to construct are the chimney stacks. Mount card can again be used for these. Once the stacks have been constructed (see Chapter 3), they can be fixed into the roof. They have been purposely made taller to fit through the roof. Cut into the profile and through the roof panels and covering using a sharp knife. Position the stacks and secure them with glue. The chimney top is created using white metal pots from the Langley range, then fixed and secured.

The stacks require the same skin finish as the walls; this is applied in the same way. The top is finished with a flaunching made up from DAS modelling clay.

## THE ROOF COVERINGS AND DETAILS TO THE EXTENSIONS

The roof covering to both extensions is made using slates created from card, fitting them in the way described in Chapter 3. The extensions will require guttering fixing to them. The main thatched roof will not require any guttering, as the large overlap on the thatch would allow the rainwater to run off clear of the walls.

## PAINTING, WEATHERING AND FINAL DRESSING

The next stage is to paint the cottage, starting with the cob walls. Mix Titanium White oil paint with a very small amount of Naples Yellow. Apply the first coat as a wash, then add a thicker consistency of paint until the desired effect is achieved, matching the prototype as far as possible. To finish off the walls, paint a near-black colour around the footing to replicate the 45cm of damp-proofing. Paint the chimney stacks in the same colours as the walls.

You can now paint the thatch; careful observation will guide you to the correct colour to use. Thatch soon weathers down to a brownish grey. Unless you want to model your cottage just after a re-thatch you will need to replicate this colour. A good base colour can be achieved by mixing Burnt Umber, Payne's Grey, Naples Yellow and Titanium White. As with the walls, start with a wash, then add thicker coats. If the thatch appears too dark at first, just go over it with some white to lighten it.

Once you are happy with the results of painting the thatch, you can paint the roofs to the extensions. These are covered with slates, so you need to start with a basic dark grey. Mix this from oil paint rather than using a spray, as the roof area to be covered is only a small amount. Pick out some of the slates in darker and lighter shades as before, creating a random pattern. Go over this again and blend them together to complete the effect.

The last items to be painted will be the doors and any guttering and downpipes fitted to the extensions. You can now add the weathering and finally some dressings to the cottage. This cottage will only require a light weathering.

*This photograph shows the colour and texture of a well-worn thatch on a cottage at Lulworth Cove, Dorset. Also worth noting is the crumbling render to the walls. A cottage such as this is full of rural character and is a very good reference for modelling this type of building.*

ABOVE: *Another photograph to illustrate the colour of thatch, this time a cottage with a straw hat in Cadgwith Cove on the Lizard Peninsula, Cornwall.*

BELOW: *The Devon cob cottage is almost now complete. The walls and the thatch have all been painted and weathered. You will notice that a black pitch damp coursing has been added to the base of the walls. This is still a common feature on the cottages found in Devon and other counties of the South-West.*

*The completed model of the Devon cob cottage is now set into the cobbles surrounding it. Roses growing over the door have been added to finish the effect.*

## SETTING THE MODEL INTO THE SCENERY

The same techniques are used here as described in the first project. Cut a footprint into fibre board to create the foundation for the cottage to fit snugly into. This cottage would be directly up to the road at the front, so add some DAS clay in front and when dry scribe some of the cobbles that are evident in a number of the photographs. Sprinkle some fine sand into a bed of dilute PVA, to represent the road surface. Once this has set, paint both the cobbles and the road's mettled surface. This now brings us to the completion of the second project.

## DERELICT LIMESTONE FIELD BARN

### REFERENCE AND PRODUCING A WORKING DRAWING

The prototype for this project stands on Bonsall Moor in Derbyshire; it is one of the many limestone field barns to be found in this part of the country. A derelict, rather than complete, barn has been chosen for this project, due to the inspirational rustic qualities it has to offer. In fact, most of the barns to be found on the moor are in this condition. A visit was made to carry out a field study, after permission from the landowner had been granted. The necessary reference information was gathered together, including measurements, a field sketch and plenty of photographs. Back at home, the information was put together to prepare a working drawing, ready to construct the model based upon it.

ABOVE: *This is the prototype for the last project, the derelict field barn.*

BELOW: *The working drawing is the basis from which the model can be created.*

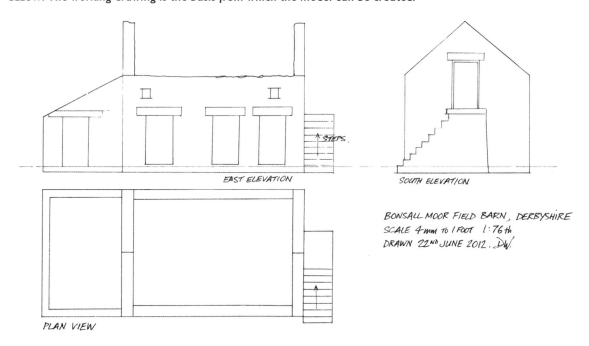

## CONSTRUCTING THE SHELL

With the drawing complete, it is time to transfer all the elevations on to the material. Foamboard is used once again, but this time 6mm (in 4mm scale) to represent the thickness of the stone walls. With the barn being a ruin, the walls are all exposed to reveal their thickness. Lay the cut-out components in order ready for assembly. One extra part to this building is the open stone steps on one gable end leading up to serve the hayloft. These have been cut out from offcuts of 3mm foamboard and assembled together, overlapping each other to produce the risers and treads.

The sides and gable ends can now be constructed and the lean-to added. Once complete, all that is required is to attach the steps at that end of the building, then add texture to them. On the prototype, there is a dip where farmers have trodden for over 200 years. This can be achieved by pushing a finger into the centre of the tread on the step; the foamboard allows this with ease.

*The components are all cut out to construct the main walls to the barn.*

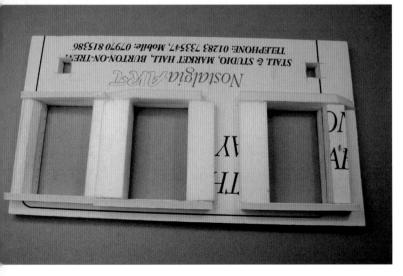

*This photograph shows the inside of the front elevation to the field barn. I have purposely added extra strips of foam board to replicate the thickness of the walls. You can clearly see where the reclaimed foam board has been used from an old display panel. If you can obtain the materials in this way, it can prove to be a very cheap way to produce a model.*

The process of constructing the steps for the barn. The steps are made from offcuts of 6mm foamboard. They are arranged to fit one on top of the other, leaving the tread of the step at one end, until the landing has been reached.

In this photograph the steps have been fixed into position on the gable end of the barn to give the farmer access to the hayloft.

To make the steps look more authentic, a worn-down dip is pushed into them. Shown here is the process of creating the dips by pressing down in the centre of the foamboard with a finger.

*Photo: Dave Richards*

*The face and all the treads of the steps, not forgetting the landing, are all given a coat of the filler plaster to create the texture and finish of limestone.*

Photo: Dave Richards

## APPLYING THE SKIN TO CREATE THE STONE

With this building being mainly constructed from rubble limestone, DAS clay is used, although for some of the inside exposed walls and to coat the steps No More Cracks is used as well. Brush the plaster on to the steps to give them a stone texture. A liberal coating of both materials is required to represent the rough stone, with the plaster being blobbed on to the inside walls. On this building the clay needs to be applied to the tops of the walls that have been left exposed; as with all the models, this needs to be left to dry off for at least twenty-four hours.

## SCRIBING THE STONEWORK

Once everything is dry, you can start to scribe the stonework, following the method described in Chapter 3. Start with corner quoins and the lintels over the doors. These need to be regular and straight, so draw them in first using a ruler or square. When you are happy with the result, move on to the rubble infill. Follow the pattern from the reference, though you can be fairly loose with your scribing technique here.

Once the sides are complete, scribe the inside walls and all the tops of the exposed walls. You can go one stage further here by carving into the clay and the foamboard underneath to create the rough, worn-away stones. It is not necessary to be too precise; after all, the building is derelict and slowly falling down. For this reason, you do not have to produce any windows or doors for your model. Neither do you have to worry about a roof, as it has long since collapsed and fallen into the structure. The next stage is to move swiftly on to the painting and the weathering.

*The walls are seen here fully scribed, starting with the quoins and the lintels. The rubble stone is scribed next; with the barn having the inside and the tops of the walls exposed, these will all have to be scribed. The stones on top of the walls are carved on the edge to give that total distressed look.*

## PAINTING AND WEATHERING

Usually the first coat of colour wash would be applied before fitting the windows, doors and roof, but in this case as none of these remain intact, everything can be painted at the same time. A dark grey wash of oil colour is applied first to represent the gaps between the stones. This wash coat soon dries, allowing the stones to be picked out using a drier mix of paint. The consistency is the same as explained in Chapter 3 for painting stonework. Be patient and try to match the colours to those in your photographs.

The quoins and lintels are made from a gritstone, so a light brown ochre colour will be required. The rest is of grey limestone, but be aware of other colour shades that are visible within this rock.

The final stage is to weather the ruin. Rain staining can be picked out and the exposed walls have a fair amount of lichens growing on them. All the techniques for applying these have been dealt with, but basically be observant and use the colours, mediums and techniques described here and you should be rewarded with a reasonable-looking model.

*The first coat of paint is added; the wash of oil colour has been made up to match the gaps between the stones.*

*The finished model of the derelict barn. The walls have now all been painted and weathered to replicate the limestone, with the quoins and lintels picked out in the colour of the Derbyshire gritstone.*

# CHAPTER SEVEN

# IMPROVING KITS AND OFF-THE-SHELF MODELS

Off-the-shelf models have been around from the 1920s or before, while kits of rural buildings have been available to use on our model railways since the 1950s. The early form of models would have been of the tinplate variety, produced for the tinplate train set. Other buildings would include farm sets made for children to play with and populate with lead farm animals. All of these early models, however, were very crude with lithographed printed windows, tiles and other features.

This chapter will concentrate on kits and off-the-shelf models from more recent times, with all the samples being created for the OO gauge model railway. We will start by taking a look at the kits that have been available over the last five decades.

## KITS FOR RURAL BUILDINGS

There were kits back in the 1950s that were produced and marketed under the name of Bilt-Eezi. They were printed on to sheets of card from origi-nal, very well designed and executed artworks. The range was vast, with most being for the line-side and urban scene. However, a good number of rural buildings made it on to the market. There were some excellent examples, obviously taken from prototypes somewhere.

The artwork was superb, but all the detail would have to be printed flat on to the sheet of card. After all these years, they are in fact still available today – I acquired some sheets from Freestone Models only a few years ago. One reason I am so fond of this range is because my very first kit-built effort, aged only six, was the Bilt-Eezi thatched cottage, built with the help of my father. These early card kits were of the fold-up design, with tabs supplied to glue the components together to construct the model. The card material was very flimsy if not backed up using thicker card or balsa wood.

The models were very good for their time and can still be seen gracing model railways. I have seen the occasional layout at recent exhibitions with one

*Pictured here is one of the vast range of Bilt-Eezi card construction kits, which have been around since the 1950s. This particular sheet contains the two thatched cottages.*

or two examples and they do not look completely out of place, especially if placed at the back of the layout where relief detail is not important.

The plastic-injected moulded kit first arrived in the late 1950s and early 1960. The likes of Kitmaster, Revel and especially Airfix started to produce buildings for the model railway market, although, again, most were of railway architecture. They did eventually produce some rural buildings including a thatched cottage, a country hotel, a church and a windmill. The Airfix thatched cottage has been chosen to make improvements to, later in this chapter.

The Superquick range of card kits made its appearance in the early 1960s. This time, although still printed flat, the card was much sturdier than that used for Bilt-Eezi kits. The Superquick samples came pre-cut, making them a little easier for the beginner to cope with. Another improvement came in the form of cut-out apertures for the windows and doors. The window frames, with glazing bars, were printed on to sheets of clear celluloid. When these were cut out they could be glued or taped into position in the ready-cut aperture, making them look more authentic. Doors, although printed flat, would also be fixed from behind the walls, giving a more three-dimensional feel to the model. The Superquick range is still very popular, but, like any pre-printed card kit, it lacks the relief and texture of the building material.

Other card kits have been produced over recent years, for example Prototype Models and the more recent Metcalfe Models. Both have followed the style of Superquick, with the die-cut printed-card method of producing model buildings, although Metcalfe has used embossing to attempt some relief and texture to the surface of the card.

Plastic-injected moulded kits have made an appearance. Ratio Models have been producing many kits of model buildings. However, the range has concentrated on the railway line-side building rather than anything of rural origins. The advantage of the plastic kit is the ability to recreate the relief and texture to the surface.

Wills produces a number of rural building kits, plus a range of building panels in plastic with a variety

*Here are a few of the many styrene building sheets produced by Wills Finecast Kits, now part of Ratio Plastic Models.*

of building materials reproduced on to the surface. These are designed to assist the scratch-builder in being creative. Wills also provides plans for some rural building using these sheets. The moulded panels are good, but they do tend to be too small and too thick. The plastic is also hard, making them very difficult to cut, especially if trying to cut out any window apertures. The Wills building range also offers window frames and doors, as well as guttering, downpipes and even chimney pots, which can be incorporated into scratch buildings if appropriate.

## OFF-THE-SHELF MODEL BUILDINGS

There has always been a market for off-the-shelf buildings to add to our model railway layouts, for those who want instant results. However, the ready-to-plant building does rather take all the fun out of the hobby. The whole idea of model railways as a hobby is to be creative and produce something in miniature for yourself. That said, there are certainly some very impressive model buildings on the market today and a lot of us might well be tempted by them.

The earliest examples of rural buildings I can recall were those few supplied by Tri-ang Hornby.

Two that come to mind are an oast house and a barn; they may have been made of rubber and perished, as they have not been seen around for a long time. There have been a few others, although most have represented the continental building rather than anything British.

There has been a definite gap in the market until recent times. The two largest businesses now competing in the model railway market have flooded us with new ranges of off-the shelf buildings, including plenty of rural examples. All come ready painted and sometimes even weathered.

Both Hornby and Bachmann UK have created these in the last ten years or so. Hornby was the first introducing the Skaledale range, but this was closely followed by Bachmann's Scenecraft buildings range. The Scenecraft range extends to those introduced and exclusive to The Model Centre (TMC), covering Heartbeat Country. It is one of these models, The Birch Hall Inn, which will be worked upon. More recently some of the famous Pendon Museum buildings have been introduced, including a replica in resin of The Waggon & Horses Pub, the very first model built for Pendon by its founder, the late Roye England.

Hornby has created a good number of new models recently, including a few that are left unpainted, so it is one of these has been chosen to work, extend and hopefully improve upon. At least this range of unpainted buildings gives the modeller something to do.

There are other ready-made rural buildings on the market, mainly cast in resin or plaster. The last building that has been picked out to improve is one of the plaster-cast samples, in 2mm scale for a change. Its origins are unknown, as it was picked up from the second-hand table in the local model shop.

There will no doubt be many more rural off-the-shelf models in the future, especially from the 'big two', Hornby and Bachmann UK. No doubt those of you reading this book would agree that ultimately the most fun and satisfaction are gained by building the model yourself. However, there is also a satisfaction to be gained from improving a kit or ready-made model and following are descriptions of work that was carried out on the kits/off-the-shelf models.

## IMPROVING A KIT – THE AIRFIX THATCHED COTTAGE

In order to show how to improve a kit, the well-established model of a rural thatched cottage has been chosen. This was originally produced by Airfix, but now belongs to Dapol. It is not a bad kit, but there is scope for improvement to make it a better model.

After removing the parts from the pack and cutting them from the sprues, the parts will require cleaning up. I decided to roughen up the panels, between the timber frames, with sandpaper to create a key for adding plaster to this area.

The next job was to give all the components of the model a base undercoat, using Halfords Plastic Filler Primer Spray for this. Once dry, some PVA glue was brushed on to the panels, followed by a coating of No More Cracks filler plaster. This gave a more realistic-looking effect, rather than the plain flat surface of the plastic.

The windows provided with the kit looked far too bulky, so I decided to keep the doors but bin the windows and make my own. After looking through my collection of photographs of similar thatched cottages, I found some that would suit. The casement frames were made up using card for the frames as described in Chapter 3. With all the windows made up, they were fixed into position using double-sided adhesive tape. Net curtains were placed behind the windows. It is easier to fix these before assembling the walls. The nets were made using tissue paper cut to size and glued in, as described earlier.

The next job before assembly was to paint the plaster panels and the timber frame. Oil paint was used again. The plaster panels were painted using a mix of Yellow Ochre, Naples Yellow and Titanium White. This gave the cream colour I was trying to replicate from a photograph of the prototype. With the panels dry, the timber frames could be painted next. Burnt Umber, Payne's Grey and a little Titanium White were mixed and applied using a small (one stroke) brush.

This is the pack containing the old Airfix plastic kit of the thatched cottage. I picked this kit to improve as it is well known, having been around for about five decades. The kit now belongs to Dapol.

The parts removed, ready for cutting away from the sprues and cleaning up.

After all the parts had been cleaned up, they were given a coat of Halfords Plastic Filler Primer Spray.

After painting, a little extra work can be carried out again before assembly. By scratching into the plaster painted panels with the tip of the scalpel, cracking effects can be created. I then used a light grey pencil crayon to go over the timber frame to give the wood the sun bleached effect. With all the sides painted and treated I could move on to assemble the basic parts to this kit.

*The gable end of the cottage with the double-sided tape in position to take the replacement windows. I decided to make them, rather than use the ones supplied.*

*The sides were given the same treatment.*

*The next job was to coat the panels between the timber frames, with the filler plaster. The plastic surface here was too clean and flat, so I roughened up the panels first, using sandpaper to create a bonding key for the PVA and plaster.*

In this photograph all the sides and ends have the plasterwork complete and the windows were being fitted. I used the card strip option, working with them flat. I started with assembling the frames direct on the positioned glazing material.

The original window frames were discarded as they seemed far too bulky for the scale of the kit. The original doors were kept, though.

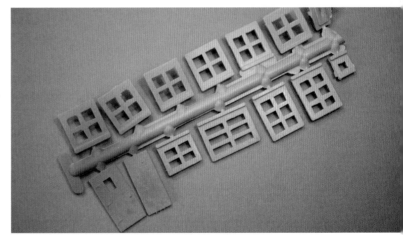

This picture illustrates the making up of the card replacement window frames. Photographs were used to copy a relevant style that would look right for this cottage. The glazing bars were cut from adhesive-backed paper labels.

Like the scratch built-farmhouse in the first project, I decided to paint the plaster panels and the timber frames before assembling the kit together.

With the wall sections all painted and the windows complete, net curtains were fitted on the back. These were made from strips of tissue paper, glued into place. I also scratched into the plaster panels with the scalpel to show a little cracking to make it look more authentic.

This photograph shows clearly how the glazing and curtains were assembled on to the reverse side of the components.

*The main wall components are shown here laid out ready to be lightly weathered.*

*I used a light grey pencil crayon to go lightly over the timber work to give that aged look. You can use chalk for this or oil pastels would also work well.*

*This close-up of the side of the cottage shows the timber work before the weathering treatment.*

*Here the treatment has been applied. It just takes the colour back and looks more authentic.*

A liquid polystyrene cement was used to glue the parts together – this gives more control and a neater finish to the model. With all the walls constructed, the roof panels can be fitted and glued into place, although the thatch has been produced moulded on to the plastic panels. It looks too regimented and hard, which is a problem with this material. To make an improvement to the roof I decided to try to thatch it using plumber's hemp. By cutting the hemp into bundles, I then fixed them to the roof panels using PVA glue. The bundles were put on in exactly the same way as on the Devon cob cottage (*see* Chapter 6), but without the staples. The whole thatch was then trimmed with scissors to finish. I

*Once the weathering treatment had been completed, the sides and ends could be assembled together.*

The roof panels were the next items to go on, although I was not happy with the original plastic thatch, so decided to try using the plumber's hemp to improve the look.

*Photo: Dave Richards*

Starting on the bottom left-hand corner the first bundle of hemp was glued into place using plenty of PVA.

*Photo: Dave Richards*

This finished thatch using plumber's hemp. The first wash coat of paint and the weathering have been applied.

One side of the roof has been left purposely showing the original plastic thatch. This was done in order to show the comparison between the hemp thatch and the plastic thatch. I am sure you will agree that the plumber's hemp has improved the look of the thatch, giving it a much more natural and realistic texture than the hard plastic surface could offer.

was very satisfied with the results – the hemp certainly improved the look of the roof and gave a more realistic result.

From reference photographs in books I noticed that most of the cottages had a lean-to extension. This may have been added later as the material did not match the timber frame and plaster infilled panels of the cottage. I decided to use a Wills styrene building panel to construct this extension.

The lap planking was selected to match an extension for which I had a reference. The components were marked and cut out, although, as mentioned earlier, the cutting of this material was not an easy task. With all the components eventually cut out, the extension was assembled together. Before adding it to the cottage, it was given a coat of red oxide primer. The extension could now be glued and secured to the main building. A roof was fabricated using the corrugated metal sheeting; the embossed styrene sheet produced by Evergreen was eventually chosen for this, as I felt that the Wills corrugated panels would appear too thick on this model.

The chimney stack was built up to a higher level than supplied in the kit. It was fabricated using mount card, then coated with the filler plaster to match the panels on the walls. The top of the stack was

finished with a card ridge to the actual top. Two white metal chimney pots finished the stack, with flaunching added around them using a little DAS clay.

My attention now turned to the final painting and weathering. First, the colour was matched and the chimney stack was painted the same as the plaster wall panels. Next, the roof was painted using oil paint, again a mix of Burnt Umber, Yellow Ochre and Payne's Grey, with some Titanium White to lighten. This produced a well-worn and sun-bleached thatch. The extension was painted using a reddish-brown colour, which was mixed using Indian Red and Yellow Ochre for the timber sides; the roof was painted dark grey. The last things to be painted were the chimney pots and the cement flaunching. For the pots, Indian Red was used and for the cement flaunching, a light grey colour, made up from Payne's Grey and Naples Yellow.

All that remained was to finish weathering the model. The thatch had already been weathered and the walls toned down before the cottage walls were assembled together, so just the extension and the chimney stack required work. The extension was toned down using Naples Yellow and Titanium White, dry-brushed on to give the effect of the timber bleaching (timber planking painted red is prone to

*The finished result. A lean-to extension made from Wills lap boarding sheets was added to the chimney end. The chimney stack was extended slightly and two pots added to complete them. To finish off, the model was mounted on to a board and final dressings applied, including roses growing around the door.*

bleaching in the sun). After this, a dirty grey-brown colour was mixed from Payne's Grey, Burnt Umber and Yellow Ochre. This was then dry-brushed on to represent the build-up of grime around the base of the timber. Turning to the corrugated roof, a small amount of Warm Red and Chrome Orange was mixed to represent rusting along the edge. The chimney just needed a light coating of the grime colour mix to soot-stain the pot and top of the stack.

All the improvements to this plastic kit were now complete. I hope you will agree that with a little extra work, as well as careful painting and weathering, a basic kit can be completely transformed.

I then took this model kit one stage further, adding final dressings to give it a more rustic feel. Plants were added, growing up around the door and to the right-hand corner. This was achieved by using Woodland Scenics foliage flock matting teased to

the desired amount and attached to the walls using a little PVA glue. The cottage was then fixed to a base with irregular cobbles scribed into a thin skin of DAS and painted to replicate the colour of cobbles. A photographic reference was found for this in my collection.

## IMPROVING AN OFF-THE-SHELF MODEL (I) – THE HORNBY (SKALEDALE) DERELICT THATCHED COTTAGE

This model comes as a complete resin shell, with the windows blocked in and a decaying thatch to the roof. The resin casting is well produced and detailed, but Hornby has given you the opportunity to paint and weather it yourself. I took the model a few stages further to add more to its rustic appeal.

*This is the resin derelict thatched cottage by Hornby as it comes bought off the shelf.*

*The first job was to give the whole model a coat of Halfords Plastic Filler Primer Spray.*

*No More Cracks filler plaster was tried out to see if it would take to the resin.*

Before any construction commenced, I gave the whole building a coat of Halfords Plastic Filler Primer Spray, to act as a key to take the oil paint. Next, I decided to improve the thatch. Although the resin thatch is good, it still lacks texture, with the material having a hard finish. Plumber's hemp would provide a softer, more natural texture. This was applied in the same way as always, putting on layers of hemp bundles from the eaves and working up to the ridge, before fixing them into position using PVA glue. I was very satisfied with the final result, especially where I had purposely put the thatch on roughly to represent where it was falling away from the roof.

The next stage of construction was to improve the boarded-up doors and windows, using a more realistic material than the resin ones provided. For this, embossed styrene sheets produced by Evergreen were used. A mixture of the vertical planked boarding and the corrugated metal sheeting was chosen. I also cut some individual planks, which were then superglued over the original resin ones provided.

I also decided to add a chimney pot to one of the tall stacks, opting for a round white metal one from Langley Models. To make it look more authentic for a derelict building, I purposely put it on at a slight angle, giving it a lean rather than being straight.

Looking through my collection of photographs I found a picture of a derelict and dilapidated farm shed. This gave me the idea to add something like this to the cottage as a lean-to cart shed or garage. Evergreen embossed sheets were again used to manufacture this, along with some strip material – I chose the 2 × 2mm to represent the framework. I first cut out the two sloping sides and back section from the vertical boarded sheet. Before adding the framework to it, I cut some gaps to represent the boards that had been broken and fallen away from the structure. Before fixing the frame to the sides, I roughened up the surface to some of the boards to replicate the rotting of the timber. This was achieved by simply scraping and scratching into the surface of the styrene with the scalpel to give it a distressed look. The framework was then attached to the inside of the sheet material using liquid polystyrene cement. Parts of the frame would, of course, be visible through the gaps in the planking; this would make it look more authentic.

The doors were made up from the same vertical planked sheet, with battens cut to size from individual planks. The doors were fixed up to the main structure, leaning one of them in a half-open position and at a slight angle, as if it was hanging off its hinges.

With the sides built and doors added, all that remained was to fit a roof. I marked out some Evergreen corrugated embossed sheet and cut it into sections to represent each sheet. The prototype sheets would be around 120 × 60cm. These were then glued into place using the liquid polystyrene cement. Again, to give a derelict look some of sheets were purposely left off, to represent those that had been ripped away either by the wind or by vandals. Some of the styrene sheets were bent at the corners to make them look even more authentic. The lean-to extension was left as a separate unit until it had been painted; it could then be fixed up to the main building.

With all the construction improvements now made, it was down to the painting, adding the render and weathering the model. I started with the walls, mixing up a brick colour from Warm Red, Yellow Ochre and Titanium White. This was dry-brushed over the raised brickwork of the casting. When the paint had dried enough, I used some of the powder residue that was a result of scribing out the DAS clay. The powder was brushed over the brickwork, letting it fall and settle into the mortar gaps. To keep the powder in place, it was given a coating of artist's fixative spray (make sure this is done in a well-ventilated room). Individual bricks were then picked out in dark grey and white.

The original casting of the cottage only had a brick infill to the timber frame. I decided to make this more rustic by adding some render over the brickwork, although only picking out sections and not adding it to the whole model. The idea was that, with the cottage being in a dilapidated state, most of the rendered skin would have fallen away to reveal the brickwork underneath.

For the render, I used both DAS modelling clay and No More Cracks filler plaster, applied with PVA

*No More Cracks successfully adhered to the resin, so I could turn my attention to painting the brickwork.*

*With the brickwork now mostly painted in, I decided to try using the DAS to replicate the plaster render, but first it was necessary to apply PVA to enable the clay to adhere to the resin shell.*

Photo: Dave Richards

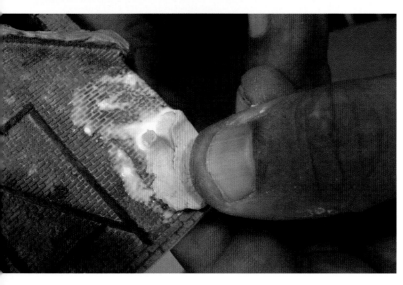

*The DAS clay was applied in the usual way, pushing it into the PVA on the walls.*

Photo: Dave Richards

*The DAS clay was added to the ends as well as the sides to recreate what was left of the plaster rendering.*

*When dry, the clay was scratched into on the surface to give the texture of the prototype.*

Photo: Dave Richards

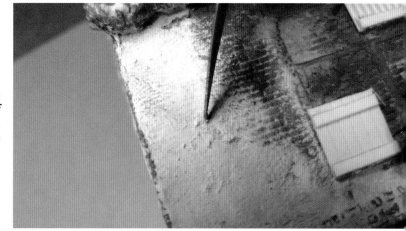

*The powdered debris was brushed away with an old toothbrush.*

Photo: Dave Richards

More scratching of the clay with the scalpel was required to replicate the cracks. Also, some of the residue powder was rubbed into the brickwork.

Photo: Dave Richards

With the cracking effect now completed, the plaster render could be painted. I used a wash mix of the oil colour to achieve the right result.

Photo: Dave Richards

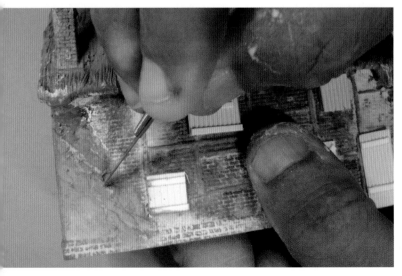

A little more scratching with the scalpel was done after the paint had dried off, in order to replicate the fresh cracking away of the render.

Photo: Dave Richards

*The finished effect, which I felt was very convincing.*

Photo: Dave Richards

*I went a stage further here and added some foliage mat to see what it would look like.*

Photo: Dave Richards

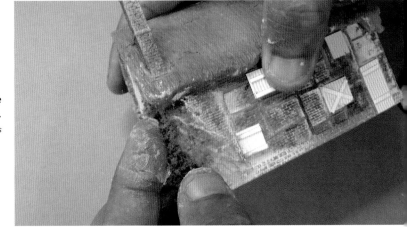

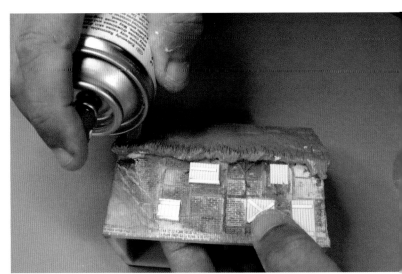

*The foliage mat worked well, so it was fixed into position using spray adhesive.*

Photo: Dave Richards

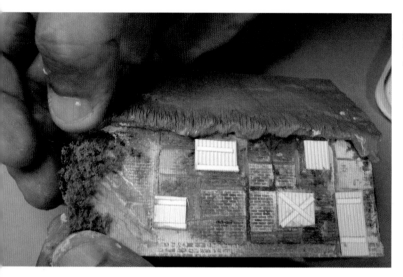

*Fixing the foliage into position; I looked at photographs I had taken of ivy growing up the corner of buildings for reference.*
Photo: Dave Richards

*A close-up of the ivy in position.*
Photo: Dave Richards

to selected sections of wall. After the plaster and DAS had dried, I worked on the surface using the tip of the scalpel blade, scratching into it to recreate the cracking away of the render. Once happy with the effect created, the render was then painted with a wash of oil colour made up from Naples Yellow and Titanium White.

The oak timber frame was the next item to be painted, using Payne's Grey for the first coat, applied using a No. I brush. I went over this again with a little Titanium White, to give the wood the bleached appearance that old untreated timber takes on. The rest of the timber was given the same treatment, although some Naples Yellow was also added to the mix for the timber on the boarded-up windows and doors. The corrugated panels were painted with a mix of Indian Red and Payne's Grey for a base colour to the metal. I went over the wooden boards with a little white, to represent the bleaching again. Chrome Orange was added to the edges of the corrugated metal sheets to represent the fresh rust appearing on them.

With the sides of the cottage now painted and weathered, the thatched roof could be tackled. A mix of Burnt Umber, Payne's Grey, Yellow Ochre, Naples Yellow and Titanium White was used again to create the main colour. This then was applied thinly over the hemp and allowed to soak into the material. It was necessary to add more white to achieve the decaying appearance of this particular thatch. To finish the thatch off, mosses were added (see Chapter 3), using Terre Verte and Sap Green.

The chimney stacks were tackled in the same way as the brickwork to the main walls. The pot was painted a cream colour, using Naples Yellow and Titanium White, then both the stacks and the pot were soot-stained and weathered down using

Payne's Grey. To finish the chimney some flaunching made from DAS clay was added around the pot.

This completed the painting and weathering to the main structure. Now I turned my attention to the painting of the lean-to garage or cart shed. The first thing to do was to give the styrene building a coat of the primer spray. The same colour was mixed for the planked boarding and the frame as was used for the boarding over the windows. This colour provided the base for all the woodwork on the outside, but I also painted the inside the same colour, as sections would be clearly visible through all the holes, gaps and where the roof panels had been removed.

*I decided to use the plumber's hemp again to improve the look of the thatch produced on the resin. It had worked fine on the plastic roof, so it should be no problem fixing it to the resin. Pictured is the finished result, which I think looks the part. The thatch was put on rather haphazardly to achieve the dilapidated and decaying state that an abandoned roof would have.*

*This close-up illustrates the haphazard application of the thatch.*

The woodwork was then dry-brushed with Titanium White to bleach it.

Looking at the photograph of the derelict shed, I noticed that the bottom of the planks, especially on one side, had green algae growing on the face of the boards. This was replicated on the model by painting on some Sap Green in those areas affected. This nicely finished off the weathering to the sides of the lean-to.

Now the corrugated roof panels could be painted. The base colour again was the same as used for the metal panels over the windows, a mix of Payne's Grey and Indian Red. After this had dried off, a little Chrome Orange was added for the fresh rust again, although this time patches on the surface were picked out as well as those at the edge.

The lean-to extension was left for a day to dry before it was fixed to the main cottage using super-glue. To set the building off, it was placed on a base of plywood, again secured with superglue. The base was then covered with a mixture of scenic materials, including carpet underlay felt, teddy bear fur and the Woodland Scenics flock and foliage mat. The felt and fur were painted to represent the overgrown state of the cottage surrounds. The ivy had been added to part of the cottage at an earlier stage, but when setting the cottage into the scenery I decided to have the ivy creeping over part of the roof and

*A close-up of the left-hand corner, with the ivy and weathering all adding to the effect.*

*The cottage model is now almost complete.
Just a few more added details are required.*

*Another view of the left corner of the cottage.*

*The first detail was to add a chimney pot,
but due to the dilapidated state of this
building I purposely fixed it on at an angle.*

*A run-down cart shed or garage was added to the finished cottage as a lean-to. This was constructed from styrene strip and sheet material. The whole thing was given a distressed appearance, with sections broken and falling away. This was carried through to the painting and weathering stage, to give the impression of years of neglect.*

up the chimney stack. The ivy was created from the Woodland Scenics foliage mat teased away and secured to the building with PVA.

To finish off, some debris from the building was scattered amongst the nettles. Some of the sheets of corrugated metal sheeting were placed where they had landed after being ripped off the roof and some of the planks that had broken away from the side of the lean-to garage were also positioned where they had fallen. Finally, an old broken cartwheel and cast-iron barrow wheel were placed where they had been abandoned. These were painted to give an aged and distressed look, with rust and green algae growing on them.

*This view shows the roof of the lean-to with panels of corrugated sheeting missing or damaged. It also illustrates the final painting and weathering to pick out the rusting away of this material.*

I hope that you will agree that these little touches bring the model to life and a basic off-the-shelf model has been improved.

*The detail around the corner of the building is shown here. The landscaping all adds to the effect, with the ivy now extended and growing over the roof of both the cottage and the lean-to; it creeps up the chimney as well. The ripped-off sections of corrugated sheeting and planking are now scattered about amongst the weeds. Scrap and debris from this building have also been included to complete the scene.*

*The cottage is now shown set into a complete rural scene in miniature.*

# IMPROVING AN OFF-THE-SHELF MODEL (II) – THE BIRCH HALL INN (BACHMANN SCENECRAFT)

This model is one of The Heartbeat Country range and is exclusive to TMC. The resin cast model is very good and comes ready painted with fine-etched brass windows fitted. I had a close look at this model to see where, if at all, it could be improved. After studying the photographs reproduced on the box, I noticed that the whitewashed older section of the building had been built with a local rubble stone. However, the model was reproduced in a dressed stone pattern, the same as the later three-storey extension, presumably to make the casting easier to produce.

I decided to set about replicating this rubble-stone finish to the old pub. To achieve this, I first brushed some PVA glue on to the surface, then by the 'blobbing' technique brushed into this some of the No More Cracks filler plaster. Scribing would be difficult with the hard resin base underneath; however, an attempt was made. Looking at the model from a distance the plaster effect without scribing did give a good enough effect.

There did not seem to be anything else required to make further improvements to the structure of the building, so it was down to painting and weathering.

The paint finish was very good and the windows and doors were finished to a very high standard. The model did fall short on the weathering, which I decided would improve the model even more. I started with the roof, adding rain-staining streaks running down the Yorkshire pantiles. Using some Payne's Grey mixed with a little Burnt Umber, a small amount was put on to the ridge tiles and

*The out-of-the-box model of The Birch Hall Inn. This fine model is produced by Bachmann UK as part of its Scenecraft range.*

*The reverse side of the model.*

then, using my finger, I dragged the paint down the tiles, making sure to keep in a straight line. The same effect was repeated where the staining would appear. Also using the same technique, streaks were applied running down from the lead flashings around the chimneys, but this time using a light grey.

The next item I added was the lichens growing on the ridge and sides of the roof covering. This was

*As a start, some filler plaster was added to the older gabled roofed section of the inn. Looking at the photographs of the building, I noticed that this side had been built from rubble stone, so decided it was worth trying to replicate this.*

Photo: Dave Richards

*First, as usual, the PVA was brushed on to the shell of the building.*

Photo: Dave Richards

*Care is needed not to get any glue on the windows and so on. Once the glue had been added, the filler plaster was brushed into it by 'blobbing' it on with a brush to replicate the raised stones.*

Photo: Dave Richards

*I thought that the roof could be improved with a little weathering, starting with the rain-staining streaks.*

Photo: Dave Richards

*Dragging a small amount of paint down from the ridge with a finger can reproduce the streaking effect quite nicely.*
Photo: Dave Richards

*The streaking is being carried out from around one of the chimney stacks. Also, to finish off the roof, lichens were added by stippling nearly dry paint on around the ridge and the edges of the roof.*
Photo: Dave Richards

applied using Chrome Orange and Yellow Ochre in the stipple technique described in Chapter 3. A few light green lichens were also added to the same areas of the roof, this time using a mix of Terre Verte and Titanium White.

I then moved on to the walls; again, careful observation of the photograph revealed the stonework of the extension had different tones within it. By mixing the colours to match the Yorkshire gritstone from Burnt Umber, Payne's Grey, Yellow Ochre, Naples Yellow and Titanium White, I was able to pick out these variations within the stonework. The gritstone also seems to weather to near-black colour. This

was evident on the ruined farmhouse on Haworth Moor, so a light dry brushing of black was added to finish the effect. To complete the walls, some rain-staining streaks were added in the areas they would appear. This was painted in the same way as those produced on the roof.

This model is now finished. Giving it a few improvements makes what is a very convincing model in the first place just a little better with that extra work. I must say that I enjoyed working on this model, as I have spent many a happy hour in the Inn, sampling their beers on visits to the North Yorkshire Moors Railway.

*The finished result. Although a well-produced and painted model in the first place, with a little more work it can be made even better.*

## IMPROVING A 2MM PLASTER-CAST BARN

This model is the plaster casting I picked up from the second-hand table in a model shop. The maker is unknown, but I liked the model. Structurally, it could not really be improved. The casting was supplied unpainted, so again it would be the painting and weathering that would improve it.

I mixed up some colour – using the same paint colours as for the Yorkshire gritstone above – for both the stone of the walls and the stone tiles covering the roof. This was applied reasonably thinly, as the plaster of the cast allowed the colour to soak into it. Once I was happy with the basic stone colour and it had dried, I then brushed the white powder residue over the stonework. This had the effect of lightening the stone, as well as filling in the mortar gaps. The model was then sprayed with the artist's fixative to hold the powder in place. The windows were picked out in dark grey using a small No. 0 brush. When dry, I carefully scratched in the glazing bars and window frames. By scratching through the paint, the white of the plaster underneath was revealed, giving a convincing fine window frame in this small scale.

The rain staining was then added to the roof and walls, but this time using a small brush to apply it. Then the lichens were added using Yellow Ochre mixed with a little Titanium White. This again was applied using a small brush. All the painting effects were the same as those used before, but with everything scaled down to look correct on a 2mm scale model.

This now concludes our look at improving kits and off-the-shelf models. If you do not feel confident enough to try a scratch-built rural building to start with, you can use these methods to have a go at improving a kit or an off-the-shelf model. Then when you are feeling more confident, you can then move on to the more adventurous projects.

This is a 2mm scale plaster cast off-the-shelf model. It is a nice model of a rural farm building. This photograph shows the 'before version'.

The finished result. Most of the improvements were made by using the various painting techniques. The stonework on the walls and stone flags on the roof were picked out and weathered to match a Yorkshire gritstone. A general weathering was then applied, with rain staining and lichens added to the roof. Last of all, the ivy was added from one of the Woodland Scenics foliage mats.

This image of a solitary old barn, dwarfed by the expanse of a summer sky, portrays how our rural buildings harmonize with, and have become an integral part of, our green and pleasant land.

# APPENDIX: COLOUR REFERENCE GUIDE

I have decided to include a quick colour reference guide. Using this Colour Reference Guide, you should be able mix the colours required to achieve realistic results when applying them to your model buildings.

All the colours used are from Winsor & Newton (Winton) or Daler-Rowney (Georgian) ranges of Artist's Oil Colours.

## WALLS BUILT FROM STONE

### DERBYSHIRE GRITSTONE
Raw Umber, Indian Red, Yellow Ochre, Naples Yellow

### YORKSHIRE GRITSTONE
Raw Umber, Yellow Ochre, Payne's Grey, Lamp Black

### YORKSHIRE AND DERBYSHIRE MILLSTONE GRIT
Indian Red, Naples Yellow, Payne's Grey

### CUMBRIAN SLATE
Terre Verte, Yellow Ochre, Vandyke Brown, Naples Yellow, Payne's Grey, Titanium White

### NORTH WALES SLATE
Permanent Mauve or Cobalt Violet Hue, Payne's Grey, Naples Yellow, Titanium White

### CORNISH AND DEVON SLATE
Terre Verte, Yellow Ochre, Burnt Umber, Payne's Grey, Naples Yellow

### CORNISH GRANITE
Raw Umber, Yellow Ochre, Payne's Grey, Titanium White

### SCOTTISH GRANITE
Payne's Grey, Permanent Mauve, Titanium White

### COTSWOLD LIMESTONE
Yellow Ochre, Naples Yellow, Titanium White

### NORTHAMPTONSHIRE LIMESTONE
Indian Red, Yellow Ochre, Titanium White

### DERBYSHIRE AND YORKSHIRE DALES LIMESTONE
Payne's Grey, Yellow Ochre, Naples Yellow, Titanium White

### SOMERSET LIMESTONE
Payne's Grey, Naples Yellow, Titanium White

### DORSET, PURBECK AND PORTLAND LIMESTONE
Burnt Umber, Naples Yellow, Titanium White

### NOTTINGHAMSHIRE SANDSTONE
Warm Red, Yellow Ochre, Naples Yellow

### DERBYSHIRE SANDSTONE
Indian Red, Raw Umber, Yellow Ochre, Naples Yellow, Titanium White

### NORFOLK FLINT
Payne's Grey, Permanent Mauve, Lamp Black

### SUSSEX, BERKSHIRE AND OXFORDSHIRE FLINT
Payne's Grey, Burnt Umber, Titanium White

### WILTSHIRE CHALK (CHILMARK) STONE
Naples Yellow, Titanium White

*Derbyshire gritstone.*

*West Yorkshire gritstone.*

*North Wales slate.*

*Mid Welsh slate.*

*Scottish granite.*

*Weathered Purbeck limestone.*

*Derbyshire limestone.*

## WALLS BUILT FROM BRICK

### COMMON RED STOCK
Indian Red, Naples Yellow; also Light Red, Naples Yellow, Titanium White

### LONDON STOCK
Raw Umber, Yellow Ochre, Titanium White

### COMMON BLUE STOCK
Payne's Grey, Permanent Mauve, Titanium White

Light red clay brick.

Multi-shade (clay) brick.

Red clay brick (with remains of rendering).

Handmade clay brick.

*Dark red and blue brick.*

*Off-white plaster render over light red brick.*

## BASIC RENDERED PLASTER AND COB

Yellow Ochre, Naples Yellow, Titanium White
   (In various parts of the country this can be painted in bright or pastel colours, such as the Suffolk Pink)

*Crumbling buff render over red brick.*

*Cream plaster over laths.*

## ROOFING MATERIALS

### COMMON WELSH SLATES
Payne's Grey, Permanent Mauve, Cobalt Blue, Titanium White

### CORNISH AND DEVON SLATES
Terre Verte, Yellow Ochre, Burnt Umber, Payne's Grey, Naples Yellow

### CUMBRIAN SLATES
Terre Verte, Yellow Ochre, Vandyke Brown, Naples Yellow, Payne's Grey

### MID WALES SLATES
Terre Verte, Vandyke Brown, Naples Yellow, Payne's Grey

### YORKSHIRE AND DERBYSHIRE LIMESTONE TILES AND FLAGS
Payne's Grey, Yellow Ochre, Naples Yellow, Titanium White

### YORKSHIRE AND DERBYSHIRE GRITSTONE TILES AND FLAGS
Payne's Grey, Yellow Ochre, Burnt Umber, Naples Yellow, Lamp Black

### PURBECK LIMESTONE TILES AND FLAGS
Burnt Umber, Naples Yellow, Titanium White

### COTSWOLD (HONEY) LIMESTONE TILES AND FLAGS
Yellow Ochre, Raw Umber, Naples Yellow

### TERRACOTTA (HANDMADE) ROOF TILES
Light Red, Vandyke Brown, Titanium White

### PLAIN CLAY TILES
Vandyke Brown, Naples Yellow

### STAFFORDSHIRE BLUE TILES
Permanent Mauve, Cobalt Blue, Payne's Grey, Titanium White

*Welsh rough-cut slate.*

*Red terracotta handmade tiles.*

*Orange pantiles.*

## COMMON TERRACOTTA PANTILES
Light Red, Vandyke Brown, Titanium White

## NORFOLK AND SUFFOLK PANTILES
Chrome Orange, Naples Yellow

## NEW AND REPLACED THATCH
Yellow Ochre, Naples Yellow, Titanium White

## OLD AND DECAYING THATCH
Raw Umber, Payne's Grey, Naples Yellow, Titanium White

## NEW CORRUGATED METAL SHEETED ROOF
Payne's Grey, Naples Yellow, Titanium White

## OLD AND RUSTING CORRUGATED METAL SHEETED ROOF
Payne's Grey, Indian Red, Naples Yellow, Chrome Orange

*Well-worn thatch.*

*Fresh orange rust.*

### NEW CORRUGATED ASBESTOS SHEETED ROOF
Naples Yellow, Payne's Grey, Titanium White

### OLD CORRUGATED ASBESTOS SHEETED ROOF
Payne's Grey, Naples Yellow, Vandyke Brown, Titanium White

### NEW TARRED ROOFING FELT
Payne's Grey, Lamp Black

### OLD AND DECAYING TARRED ROOFING FELT
Payne's Grey, Naples Yellow, Terre Verte

### FRESHLY CREOSOTED TIMBER
Burnt Umber, Lamp Black

### OLD OR SUN-BLEACHED TIMBER
Payne's Grey, Naples Yellow, Titanium White

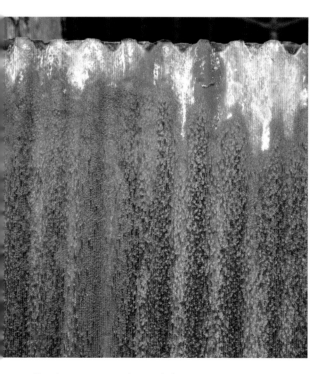

*Rusting corrugated metal sheet.*

*Sun-bleached grey-silver timber boarding.*

*Green algae on timber.*

*Orange and ochre lichens on stone.*

*Green algae on gritstone.*

## OLD, DECAYING AND DAMP TIMBER
Payne's Grey, Naples Yellow

## ALGAE GROWING ON TIMBER
Terre Verte or Sap Green

## LICHEN GROWING ON ROOF COVERINGS
Yellow Ochre, Chrome Orange or Terre Verte, Titanium White

# LIST OF SUPPLIERS

Scale rules, small squares, scalpels, blades, cutting mats, paint brushes, dentist's probes and general tools:

**Eileen's Emporium**
Unit 19
12 Higham Business Centre
Newent Road
Gloucester
GL2 8DN
Telephone: 01531 828009
www.eileensemporium.com

**Hobby Holidays**
The Spinney
Low Street
Beckingham
Nr Doncaster
South Yorkshire
DN10 4PW
Telephone: 01427 848979
www.hobbyholidays.co.uk

**Squires Model & Craft Tools**
100 London Road
Bognor Regis
West Sussex
PO21 1DD
Telephone: 01243 842424
www.squirestools.com

Foamboard, DAS modelling clay, paints, brushes, styrene sheet and strip:

**Eileen's Emporium**
(see above)

**Evergreen Scale Models, inc.**
12808 N.E. 125th Way
Kirkland, WA
98034
USA
www.evergreenscalemodels.com

**Freestone Models**
28 Newland Mill
Whitney
Oxfordshire
OX28 3HH
Telephone: 01993 775975
www.freestonemodel.co.uk

**Hobby Holidays**
(see left)

**Slater's (Plastikard) Ltd**
Old Road
Darley Dale
Matlock
Derbyshire
DE4 2ER
Telephone: 01629 734053
www.slatersplastikard.com

**Squires Model & Craft Tools**
(see left)

Scenic materials, plumber's hemp, scenic accessories:

**Dart Castings**
17 Hurst Close
Staplehurst
Tonbridge Wells
Kent TN12 0BX
Telephone: 01580 892917
www.dartcastings.co.uk

**Duncan Models**
34 Waters Road
Salisbury
Wiltshire
SP1 3NX
Telephone: 01722 321041
www.duncanmodels.co.uk

**Green Scene (Scenic Modelling & Accessories)**
60 Hollymount
Worcester
WR4 9SF
Telephone: 01905 524298
www.green-scene.co.uk

**Heki**
HEKI-Kittler GmbH
Am Bahndamm 10
D-76437 Rastatt-Wintersdorf
Germany
www.heki-kittler.de

**Langley Models**
166 Three Bridges Road
Crawley
Sussex
RH10 1LH
Telephone: 0870 0660 416
www.langleymodels.co.uk

**Malcolm's Miniatures**
14 Oakdene
Woodcote
Reading
Oxfordshire RG8 0RQ
Telephone: 01491 680951
www.malcolmsminiatures.co.uk

**S&D Models**
Highbridge Works
PO Box 101
Burnham-on-Sea
TA9 4WA
www.sanddmodels.co.uk

**Springside Models**
2 Springside Cottages
Dornafield Road
Ippleton
Newton Abbot
Devon
TQ12 5SJ
Telephone: 01803 813749
www.springsidemodels.com

**Woodland Scenics**
PO Box 98
Linn Creek
MO 65052
USA
www.woodlandscenics.com

# FURTHER INFORMATION

## REFERENCE BOOKS

*English Villages (Classic Photographs from the Francis Frith Collection)*
Published by Black Horse Books
Frith's Barn
Teffont
Salisbury, Wiltshire
SP3 5QP
ISBN 1-84546-332-3
www.francisfrith.co.uk

*In Search of a Dream – The Life and Work of Roye England*
**Edited by Stephen Williams**
Published by Wild Swan Publications Ltd
1–3 Hagbourne Road
Didcot, Oxon
OX11 8DP
ISBN 1-874103-62-3
www.titfield.co.uk/WSmain.htm

*Rural Britain (Then & Now)*
**By Roger Hunt**
The Octopus Publishing Group Limited
Endeavour House
189 Shaftesbury Avenue
London
WC2H 8JY
ISBN 1-84403-0431
www.octopusbooks.co.uk

## MUSEUMS

**Avoncroft Museum**
Stoke Heath
Bromsgrove
B60 4JR
www.avoncroft.org.uk

**Pendon Museum Trust Ltd**
Long Wittenham
Abingdon, Oxfordshire
OX14 4QD
www.pendonmuseum.com

**St Fagans National History Museum**
St Fagans
Cardiff
CF5 6XB
www.museumwales.ac.uk/en/stfagans

**The Silk Mill – Derby Museum of Industry**
Silk Mill Lane
Off Full Street
Derby
DE1 3AF

**Weald & Downland Open Air Museum**
Chichester
PO18 0EU
www.wealddown.co.uk

## ORGANIZATIONS, SERVICES AND FURTHER INFORMATION

**Dovedale Models (David Wright, DVDs and Model-Making Services)**
6 Ivy Court
Hilton, Derbyshire
DE65 5WD
Telephone: 01283 733547
www.dovedalemodels.co.uk

**English Heritage**
www.english-heritage.org.uk

**Gauge O Guild**
www.gauge0guild.com

# INDEX

# RELATED TITLES FROM CROWOOD

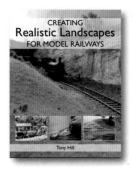

**Creating Realistic Landscapes for Model Railways**

TONY HILL

ISBN 978 1 84797 219 4

160pp, 400 illustrations

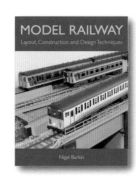

**Model Railway Layout, Design & Construction Techniques**

NIGEL BURKIN

ISBN 978 1 84797 181 4

192pp, 340 illustrations

**Planning, Designing and Making Railway Layouts in Small Spaces**

RICHARD BARDSLEY

ISBN 978 1 84797 424 2

144pp, 130 illustrations

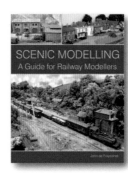

**Scenic Modelling**

JOHN DE FRAYSSINET

ISBN 978 1 84797 457 0

160pp, 230 illustrations

In case of difficulty ordering, contact the Sales Office:

The Crowood Press Ltd
Ramsbury
Wiltshire
SN8 2HR
UK

Tel: 44 (0) 1672 520320
enquiries@crowood.com
**www.crowood.com**